General Editor: Roger Whiting

CHURCHES

ROGER WHITING
Formerly Head of History, King's School, Gloucester

GRAHAM BERRY
Richmond School, Yorkshire

With additional material from
Carole Brown
Nunthorpe School, Cleveland

Stanley Thornes (Publishers) Ltd

First published in 1988 by:
Stanley Thornes (Publishers) Ltd
Old Station Drive
Leckhampton
CHELTENHAM GL53 ODN
England

British Library Cataloguing in Publication Data
Whiting, Roger
Churches. — (Footprints)
1. Great Britain. Local history.
Historical sources
I. Title II. Series
941

ISBN 0-85950-688-6

Cover illustration: Chesterfield, Derbyshire, reproduced by kind permission of Aerofilms Ltd.

Typeset by Tech-Set, Gateshead, Tyne & Wear, in 10/12 Palatino
Printed and bound in Great Britain by Ebenezer Baylis & Son, Worcester

Contents

WARNING. REMEMBER TO GET PERMISSION FROM THE OWNERS OF ANY PRIVATE LAND, OR BUILDINGS, YOU WANT TO ENTER DURING YOUR RESEARCH.

Acknowledgements

The authors and publishers are grateful to the following for supplying and giving permission to reproduce prints and artwork.

BBC Hulton Picture Library, pp. 2, 17
Dr J.H. Bettey, p. 16
M. Child, *Discovering Churchyards* (Shire Publications, 1982), photographs by Cadbury Lamb, pp. 22 (bottom), 24
P. and T. Clowney, *Exploring Churches* (Lion, 1982), p. 19 (bottom)
K.A. Esdale, *English Church Monuments* (Batsford, 1946), p. 36 (bottom left); photograph by Sidney Pitcher, p. 36 (right)
J. Harries, *Discovering Churches* (Shire Publications, 1982), p. 21; from drawings by Dennis Lack, pp. 9, 11, 12, 13, 14, 15, 29
C. Howkins, *Discovering Church Furniture* (Shire Publications, 1980), photographs by Cadbury Lamb, pp. 32 (bottom), 33 (bottom); from drawings by Christopher Howkins, p. 33 (middle left and right)
A. Jellicoe and R. Mayne, *Devon* (Shell Guide, Faber and Faber, 1975), photographs by Roger Mayne, pp. 31 (bottom), 32 (top)
A.F. Kersting, p. 29 (top)
North Yorkshire County Record Office, p. 40 (bottom)
Nottinghamshire Leisure Services (Libraries) Department, p. 1
T.M. Nye, *Parish Church Architecture* (Batsford, 1965), from drawings by architects Ansell and Bailey, p. 19 (top); from drawings by architects Braddock Martin-Smith, p. 20 (top and bottom)
C. Platt, *Parish Churches of Medieval England* (Batsford, 1965), from drawings by Dr L.A. Butler, *Proceedings of the Cambridge Antiquarian Society*, vol. 50, 1956, p. 23
H. Pluckrose, *Looking Around – Outside* (Heinemann), drawings of windows, pp. 9, 11, 12, 13, 14
Public Record Office, © Crown, p. 6
Canon M.H. Ridgway, for photograph from the collection of the late F.H. Crossley, p. 31 (top left)
W. Rodwell, *Journal of Antiquaries*, vol. 58, 1978, p. 13 (bottom)
Royal Commission on the Historic Monuments of England, pp. 10 (right), 11 (right), 14 (left), 25 (bottom), 26 (photograph by Paul Upton), 27, 30 (top and bottom), 31 (top right, middle right), 34 (left), 35, 37 (left)
E. Smith *et al*, *English Parish Churches* (Thames & Hudson, 1976), photographs by Edwin Smith, p. 18 (top and bottom)
B. Taylor, *Middle Ages* (Brockhampton Press, 1971), drawing by Valerie Bell, p. 36 (top left)
H. Taylor, *Anglo-Saxon Architecture*, vol. 3 (Cambridge University Press), p. 10 (left)
The Master and Fellows of Trinity College, Cambridge, p. 22 (top)
Elizabeth Whiting, p. 34 (right)
John Whiting, p. 37 (right)

The diagram of the church on p. 8 is adapted from L.E. Jones, *The Observer's Book of Old English Churches*, © Frederick Warne & Co., 1965, 1969, drawn by Anthony S. New.

All other prints are reproduced by kind permission of the authors.

Every effort has been made to contact copyright holders, and we apologise if any have been overlooked.

We are also grateful to:

Richmond School, Yorkshire and Nunthorpe School, Cleveland for reference to their project work.

Kate Overy of Nunthorpe School for work done by her.

And all those schools who responded to a letter from the publishers inviting information about their local history work – and whose material was helpful in providing background for the series.

1 Footprints of the Past

Sometimes history seems to be something which happens somewhere else and affects only other people. That may be true of wars and the rise and fall of governments, but there is just as much *history* on your *doorstep*. In fact the effect of warfare and the changing of governments may well have caused big changes in your locality. Your comprehensive school may well have been a grammar or secondary modern school a few years ago. The street it faces on to may refer to a time when your locality was part of the defence complex needed in times of rebellion or invasion, such as *Castle Street*, to take a random example. Your own home may have a history, or, if it is a new one, the estate on which it stands may well have a tale to tell. Odd curves in country roads or hump lines across fields were once put there for a purpose. The alterations to the local church or mill reflect the changes they had to face up to in bygone days. There is nothing to stop you becoming a *historian-detective* to find out what the story is behind so much that is around you. This series of books aims to equip you for this exciting and rewarding task.

A church's development may go back centuries or only a short time. Whether its history is long or short, a church will always have changed and developed. How such changes came about can be discovered by studying documents of different kinds and by going out on the site with a measuring tape, notebook and camera.

Any historian-detective will want to find out:

(a) What signs are there that things have changed very little? Experts call this *continuity*, that is, things continuing roughly the same down the ages.

(b) What *changes* have occurred and why?

All history is made up of a combination of continuity and change. It is fascinating to find out why some things change very little, if at all, while others change a lot.

A parish church is not simply a building; it is, or was, the centre of local activities, and we shall have to look for evidence of those activities in the structure and contents of the building. We shall also have to examine the graveyard to see what it can tell us. There is a variety of specialisations which you might choose to concentrate on: the changing patterns of Christian names on gravestones, costumes and armour as depicted on tombs, the importance of the pulpit's size and placing (and so of preaching in the services), and the various kinds of community service based at the church.

The sections of this book will introduce you to the different kinds of document you can consult if you do a parish church research project, what to look for on the ground, and how to record the evidence you find. Chapter 7 shows how two schools investigated different aspects of parish churches. Then you will be ready to do your own research.

2 Looking at a Parish Church

Sometimes, as you look at a church or walk round a graveyard, you might wonder why parish churches have been such an important feature of people's lives over the centuries. If you look at a parish magazine today it will show you that the building and its facilities are in use *all* the week, and not just for worship. In fact it caters for all ages and needs. If this is so today, when the Welfare State provides so much for those in all kinds of need, think how much more of a centre for community activity it must have been in bygone years.

The parish church was the charity centre, the news-agency, the library, the recreation centre, the distress-relief centre for the worried, the court for certain behavioural matters and wills, a place for trial by ordeal and sometimes punishment (public penance, stocks or pillory), a place of refuge in danger, the alarm centre (church bells) and the fire station, as well as the place where (with baptism and funeral) one began and ended one's life. Churches have been used as alarm centres. Molland Church, Devon, still has the notice up for what to do when Napoleon invades! In the Second World War church bells were to be used only in the event of an invasion. Today, churches like St Martins-in-the-Field, London, use their crypts to care for the homeless. Look at the church porch to see if there are any public notices there. An example in a farming area might be one on swine fever which requires the control of animals' movement. Of course there may not be any notices if none has been issued which applies in that area.

Here are some of the kinds of evidence you will need to examine in order to find out about the role of a parish church. We will look at them in more detail later.

(a) *Churches and graveyards* Tombstones and monumental inscriptions can tell you a great deal about the people who used the church. For example, the changes in architecture and fixtures, such as screens and altars, can indicate how people changed their ways of worship. See Chapters 2, 4, 5 and 7.

(b) *Documents* There is a wide variety of documents about churches, including parish registers, church-wardens' accounts, vestry minutes, the accounts of overseers of the poor, and church court records. These are just a few of the documents which can help to bring a church alive, and we will return to them in Chapters 3 and 7.

(c) *Oral history* You can try and find people connected with the local church today who can describe its role over the years. They may recall what their parents told them, or have newspaper cuttings or photographs to show you. See Chapter 6.

Do not forget to use Chapter 8 to find out what books have been written on church history.

The family goes to church, c. 1900

3 Finding and Using Documents

The types of archive mentioned in this section can be found in your county record office, local museum or library, or might possibly be in the possession of the vicar of your local church. If you study this section carefully you will know what kinds of material you may find and what it will look like when you ask for it.

PARISH RECORDS

Parish records may still be available in manuscript form in your church's parish chest, the local record office or the diocesan registry. Sometimes printed extracts have appeared in local history books or in volumes printed by a local record society. You would find these in a reference library.

PARISH REGISTERS

These registers, especially the lists of burials, can give information about parishioners who came to worship, for example their trades and occupations. The keeping of registers of baptisms, marriages and deaths was compulsory from 1538.

Below is an extract from the parish burial register of Aberford, West Yorkshire.

Burials from Lady day 1803 to Lady day 1804			*Age*
April	6	Joseph Mills, a youth at Ephraim Sanderson's school	12
	27	Joseph, son of Joseph Smith, carrier & Mary, his wife	4 months
May	1	James Clapham, warrener	60
	8	William Jackson, servant	51
	24	John, son of William Loryman, Labr & Hannah, his wife	9
	29	William Bullock, gentleman	63

CHURCHWARDENS' ACCOUNTS

Churchwardens' accounts record the changes in the fabric of the church; its reconstruction, repair, fittings, books and vestments. In the extract opposite from the 1550s, you can see how St Mary's Church, Devizes, was affected first by the new Protestantism of Edward VI's reign and then by the return to Roman Catholicism under Mary I. Make lists of those changes that you think were (a) Protestant, and (b) Roman Catholic.

1550 4 Edw. VI. Pd for their labour at the plucking down of the Altars, and for meat and drink — *xiv d*
Pd for their labour at the taking down of the side Altar — *xii d*
1553 1 Mary. Pd to Bartlett for setting up the great Altar — *viii d*
Pd to James Benett the mason for his work about the Altar — *vi d*
1554 2 Mary. Pd for holy oil — *iv d*
To Wm. Jefferies for ii tapers [candles] of a pound and a half — *xviii d*
For the new making of the same tapers against Easter — *xi d*
There is to be accounted for of old ix days work for George Tylar and his man, at vii d the day, for putting and making up of the organ loft — *v s iii d*
1555 3 Mary. Pd for defacing the Scriptures on the walls — *ii s iv d*
Pd for making of the Altar and for defacing the x commandments and putting in the Roodloft [see page 29] — *vi d*
Pd for making Mary and Joseph — *v s iv d*
1561 4 Elizabeth. For taking down of the Roodloft — *vi d*

GLEBE TERRIERS

Glebe terriers are land surveys which listed the lands of the church and the dues of the priest (see page 25). They start with a description of the church fabric, furnishings, churchyard, parsonage and any church outbuildings, cottages, etc. Here are some extracts from the Glebe Terrier of Barwick-in-Elmet, West Yorkshire, 1764:

Tythes of Wool and Lamb is all due throughout the Whole Parish and Payable in kind, but the Rector Usually agrees to take one Penny for every fleece of Wool, and Threepence for every Lamb . . .

The known Customs of the Parish for Easter Reckonings, Surplice fees and other Ecclesiastical Dues are as follows (viz.) to the Rector:

A Marriage by Licence	*10s 0d*
Banns and Publication	*3s 6d*
Churching a Woman [after childbirth]	*8d*
Registering Child's Name	*4d*
Funeral Sermon	*10s 0d*
Funeral in the Body of the Church	*6s 8d*
In the Quire [choir]	*13s 4d*
In the Churchyard	*1s 0d*
Every Communicant [person receiving Communion]	*2d*
Every House Holder, a Hen or Sixpence at Christmas	*6d*
Bees per Swarm 1d House Dues 2d	*3d*
Plough 1d Foal 1d Cow 1d Calf $\frac{1}{2}$d	*$3\frac{1}{2}$d*

VESTRY MINUTES

These deal largely with life in the parish rather than in the church itself, because the vestry was the parish 'parliament'. Here is an extract from Braintree Vestry Minutes, 1619:

Imprimis [in the first place] it is agreed that Arbinger being sent by his father back again after that by the Justices warrant he was sent from Braintree to him shall be corrected as a vagrant and be sent with a passport back again to Stebbing to his father. It is agreed that Robert Eliott being grown aged and poor shall be put into the Almshouse where Baldwin is and he turned out.

ACCOUNTS OF THE OVERSEERS OF THE POOR

The accounts opposite show how the parish overseers met in the church vestry and dealt with the poor. These extracts from the Overseers' Accounts for Barwick-in-Elmet in the eighteenth century show how the poor had to wear badges. See if you can work out the story behind their handling of Jane Hopwood.

		£	s	d
1734	Cloth for badges			7
	Pd Samuel Waite for setting them on			6
	Attending badging the poor			6
1735	For the cure of Ester Thorn's leg	2	2	0
1751	Going to Leeds to get licence for Jane Hopwood		4	6
	Paid for licence	1	7	6
	Wedding dues		15	0
	For meat and drink		15	6
	To the ringers		1	0
	A horse for John Hacksup		1	0
	Attending the wedding		1	6
	A pair of new shoes for Jane Hopwood		3	0
	Gave John Hacksup for Jane's portion		2	6
	Paid Thomas Hacksup for bringing about the wedding		10	6
	To William Thompson for carrying her goods		6	0
	Myself going with them and charges		2	6

BISHOPS' REGISTERS AND LICENCES

Bishops' registers, starting with those of Lincoln in 1209, are the oldest records. Among other things, they detail the consecration of churches and the misbehaviour of clergy. Some have been printed by the Canterbury and York Society.

Bishops' licences date from about 1500 and show clergymen's careers as well as details of licences to work given by bishops to teachers, surgeons, midwives, parish clerks and curates. Who licences such people today?

BISHOPS' VISITATIONS

These cover mainly the period from 1660 to 1860. Bishops investigated whether or not the priest was living in his parish, the value of the church plate, the church's property, the number of families in the parish, main employment opportunities, charities, almshouses, charity schools, the number of dissenters, etc. Sometimes bishops sent questionnaires to their clergy.

In 1551 Bishop John Hooper of Gloucester examined his clergy about their faith, asking them: (1) What are the articles of the Christian Faith? (2) Can you repeat them from memory? (3) Can you prove them by the authority of the Scriptures? (4) Can you recite the Lord's Prayer? (5) How do you know it was the Lord's Prayer? (6) Where was it written? (7) List the Ten Commandments. The vicar of South Cerney said the Lord's Prayer 'was given by his lord the King and written in the King's book of Common Prayer'! Here are some of the inquiry's findings from one parish:

Quinton parish: Hugh Tipping, Vicar.

(1) Commandments: Says there are ten, but knows not where written and cannot recite by memory.

(2) Articles of Faith: Knows the Articles of Faith, and recited them by memory, but gave no proof by authority of Scripture.

(3) Lord's Prayer: Can repeat the Lord's Prayer by memory and knows it is the Lord's Prayer because it was given by Christ to his apostles and is written in Matthew xi.

Of Gloucestershire's 311 clergy, 62 were found to be non-resident, 171 were unable to recite the Ten Commandments, 33 could not find them in the Bible, 30 could not find the Lord's Prayer and 27 did not know its author.

ECCLESIASTICAL COURT RECORDS

Ecclesiastical courts, such as the bishop's consistory court and the archdeacon's court, dealt with matters like immorality, blasphemy, drunkenness, neglect of duty by parish officers, non-payment of church rates, misbehaviour on Sundays, possession of 'popish' relics, use of incorrect services and vestments, unlicensed preaching, and wills and church fabric. Their *act books* summarise what happened, and their *cause* (case) *books* give full details.

The Revd William Lynche, aged 63, of Beauchamp Roothing, Essex, who had already been made to do public penance for drunkenness, appeared before the archdeacon's court in 1563 for allowing his wife to dance in a common alehouse. He stated:

That his wife has danced at the common alehouse
Item that he never willed her to dance himself
Item that he has seen other men kiss his wife after dancing in the common alehouse
Item that he has not seen any bachelor kiss her but they have danced with her
Item that he has willed her to come from the alehouse with him but she prayed him to tarry [wait].

She confessed:-
That she has danced at the common alehouse
Item that she has danced with bachelors and wild youth at that house
Item that she never kissed any bachelor in dancing
Item that she has heard herself accused of evil fame.

RELIGIOUS CENSUS, 1851

This Census covered both the Church of England and Nonconformists. Counting was careless but the facts on how the buildings came to be built and their price and capacity are accurate. It suggested that under a third of all adults went to church, but that two-thirds were members in theory. There were considerable variations: urban workers were the least interested. The average size of a Church of England congregation in 1851 was 647; by 1881 this had risen to 676.

LOCAL NEWSPAPERS

Newspapers can be invaluable sources of information about churches, as this extract from the *Cheltenham Free Press*, 2 July 1898 shows.

The people of the pretty little Cotswold village of Lower Guiting don't go to church, and, what is more to the point, they declare that they won't. The letters that have appeared in our columns during the past two months supply the reason for such a determined attitude, i.e., opposition to the vicar (Rev. J. E. Green) and his alleged ritualistic innovations in the church service.

On Monday was reported the arrival of the Bishop Hooper van in the village. The van belongs to the Church Association and National Protestant League, the aim of which is expressed in large characters upon the van as 'the maintenance of the Protestant character of the Church of England'. It professes to do this by sending lecturers into the parishes . . . where ritualism is said to be rampant, to stir up the parishioners against 'the introduction into the Church of England of the abominable practices of ritualism, confession and absolution of the Church of Rome' as the lecturers call it.

The article goes on to describe how the lecturer was confronted by the ex-curate turned monk of the parish, which led to the villagers pelting the monk with smelly missiles in a fury that lasted until after midnight!

MEMORIAL INSCRIPTIONS

Inscriptions on memorials may occasionally be helpful, like this one in Bibury Church, Gloucestershire, about the Revd Benjamin Wynnington who died in 1673. It not only tells you about the preaching customs of those days, but also how the lord of the manor regarded the vicar!

Mr Wynnington was a very laborious minister, of whom it is said, that after he had preached an hour by the glass, he would turn it, assuring the congregation, that he meant to continue in his sermon only one hour longer. And it is added, that during

246 - 2 - p. 1   4

Census of Great Britain, 1851.

(13 and 14 Victoriæ, Cap. 53.)

A RETURN

Of the several Particulars to be inquired into respecting the undermentioned CHURCH or CHAPEL in England, belonging to the United Church of England and Ireland.

[A similar Return (*mutatis mutandis,*) will be obtained with respect to Churches belonging to the Established Church in Scotland, and the Episcopal Church there, and also from Roman Catholic Priests, and from the Ministers of every other Religious Denomination throughout Great Britain, with respect to their Places of Worship.]

	NAME and DESCRIPTION of CHURCH or CHAPEL.		
I.	Saint John the Evangelist, King's Lynn, a New Parish Church (6 & 7 Victoria Chap 37)		
		Parish, Ecclesiastical Division or District, Township or Place	Superintendent Registrar's District	County and Diocese
II.	WHERE SITUATED.	New Parish of St John King's Lynn Situated in Blackfriar's Road	King's Lynn	County of Norfolk Diocese of Norwich

	WHEN CONSECRATED OR LICENSED	Under what Circumstances CONSECRATED or LICENSED
III.	September 24. 1846	As an additional Church

IV. In the case of a CHURCH or CHAPEL CONSECRATED or LICENSED since the 1st January, 1800; state

HOW OR BY WHOM ERECTED	COST, how Defrayed	
By Parliamentary Grant	By Grant for Ch. Buildg Soc.	£400
Grant from Church Build Soc	By ~~Parliamentary Grant~~ the Church Building Commiss	500
Grant from Diocesan Soc	~~Parochial Rate~~ Diocesan Ch Build Soc	100
Private Subscriptions	„ Private Benefaction, or Subscription, or from other Sources	about 5160
	Total Cost......£	6160

V. HOW ENDOWED	£		£	VI. SPACE AVAILABLE FOR PUBLIC WORSHIP	
Land		Pew Rents	about 60	Free Sittings	804
Tithe		Fees	about 5	Other Sittings	200
Glebe		Dues			
Other Permanent Endowment	150	Easter Offerings		Total Sittings...	1004
		Other Sources			

VII. Estimated Number of Persons attending Divine Service on Sunday, March 30, 1851.

	Morning	Afternoon	Evening
General Congregation	390	60	432
Sunday Scholars	175	258	—
Total..	565	318	432

AVERAGE NUMBER OF ATTENDANTS during Months next preceding March 30, 1851. (See Instruction VII.)

	Morning	Afternoon	Evening
General Congregation			
Sunday Scholars			
Total...			

VIII. REMARKS The Pew-rents are employed to defray the expenses of the Church. The afternoon service is only on the last Sunday of every month & is attended by other Scholars besides those of the Parish.

I certify the foregoing to be a true and correct Return to the best of my belief.

Witness my hand this 31st day of March 1851.

IX. (*Signature*) E. F. E. Hankinson

(*Official Character*) Perpetual Curate of the above named St John King's Lynn

(*Address by Post*) King's Lynn

Religious Census return for St John's Church, King's Lynn, 1851. When was it built and how was it paid for? Notice the reference to pew rents.

the second hour of the sermon, Mr Sackville, then lord of the Manor, usually retired from church to smoke his pipe, but always returned in time to receive the benediction.

WILLS

If you are able to examine some sixteenth-century wills, notice the change in their wording during the course of the century. In earlier, Catholic, wills people leave their souls to God and 'to the Blessed Virgin Mary and the Whole Company of Heaven', while later, Protestant ones commit them to 'Almighty God and his Only Son our Lord Jesus Christ, by whose precious death and passion I hope only to be saved'. Wills also provided for feasts in the church:

The Sunday next after her burial, there shall be provided two dozens of bread, a kilderkin [about 80 litres] of ale, two gammons of bacon, three shoulders of mutton, and two couples of rabbits, desiring all the parish, as well rich as poor, to take part thereof, and a table to be set in the middle of the church with everything necessary thereunto.

Margaret Atkinson's will, (1544)

CONTEMPORARY DIARIES AND NOVELS

The Revd James Woodforde's *Diary of a Country Parson* gives a day-by-day description of Woodforde's life in the eighteenth century. For the nineteenth century, a similar account is the Revd F. E. Witts's *Diary of a Cotswold Parson*. George Eliot's *Scenes from Clerical Life* describes an early-nineteenth-century parish, while Thomas Hardy's *Under the Greenwood Tree* deals with church orchestras and carol singing. All these books are available in reprinted editions through your public library, where you can also consult the parish history volumes of the *Victoria County History*.

FURTHER READING

Purvis, J. S. *Introduction to Ecclesiastical Records* (St Anthony's Press, 1953)
National Index of Parish Registers (Society of Genealogists, vols from 1976)

4 Evidence on the Ground

(a) The Church

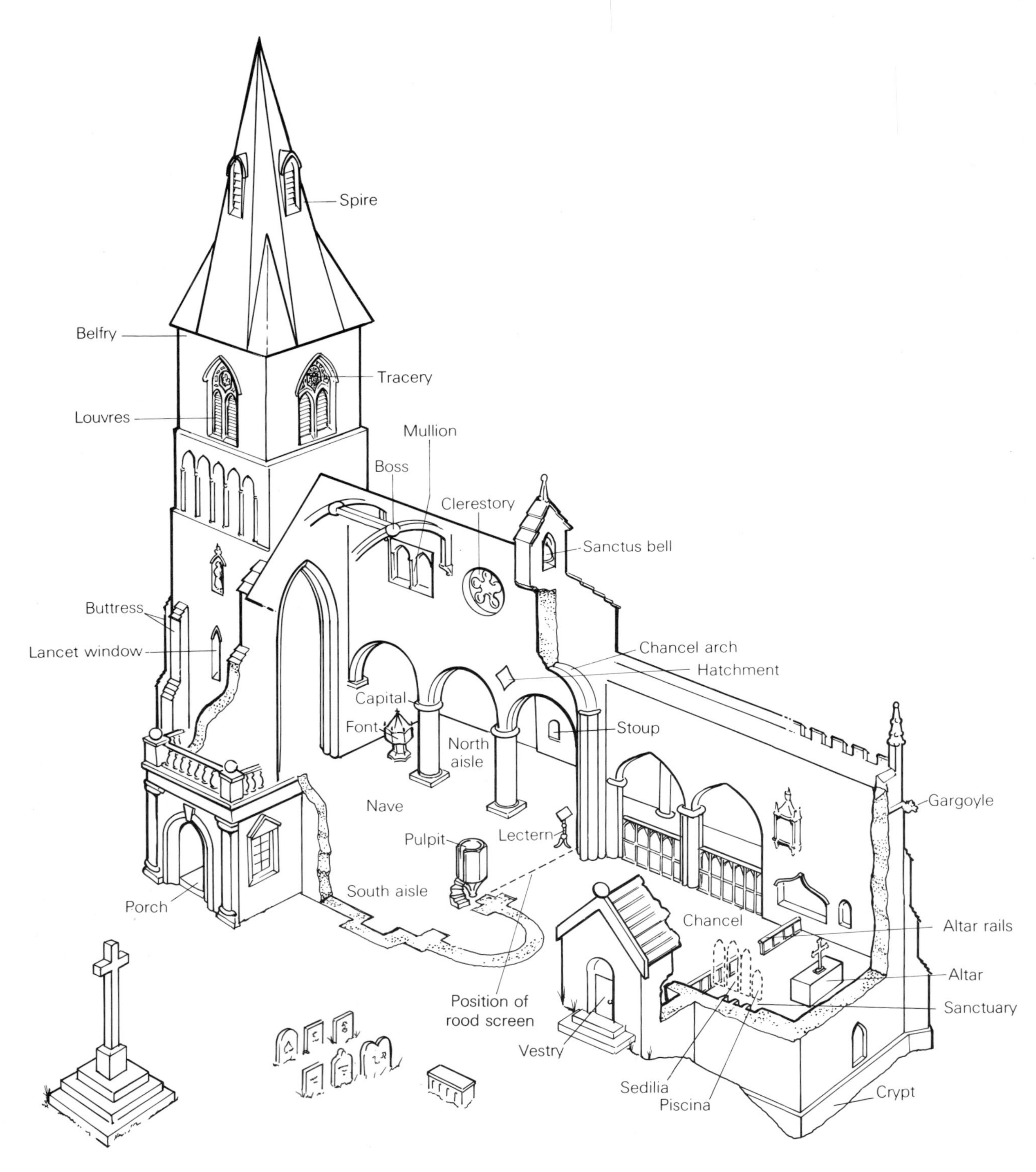

The main features of the parish church

When you first look at your parish church you may find it appears to be something of an architectural muddle. If so, it simply shows that it has been built and re-built or extended over the centuries. Parish churches are the most altered, redesigned and totally rebuilt type of building in the country. So they will vary enormously depending on when they were built, and on the parish they were designed, or adapted, to serve. It is hard to know where to begin when one walks up to such a building for the first time. Almost always there will be an easy starting point, the booklet on the bookstall giving a 'brief history of our parish church'. Inside will be a plan clearly marking the date of different building stages. Special features will be listed and explained.

Your task will be to identify what is referred to, and to try and spot the changes over the centuries. Do not forget to ask yourself why those changes proved necessary. Perhaps a fire in the wooden roof caused a rebuilding, or the enlargement of the town or village required more space for worshippers, or development in the *liturgy* (the ritual, or the way a service is conducted) required new fittings. Architects seem to be happy to introduce the latest style when rebuilding or extending a church, fitting it straight on to the old style. Sometimes you can see the old style partially hidden behind the new. Sometimes there are ugly joins between the two styles.

Because churches have changed so much over the centuries it will be best to give you information and advice in *chronological order* – that is, century by century.

SAXON PERIOD, 608–1066

You will find that the towers, walls and arches of Saxon churches were usually slender compared to Norman ones (see pages 10–11). One obvious sign of a church being Saxon is that the windows were small and fairly high up. Saxon masons also liked making patterns on their stonework – for example herringboning, which consisted of setting rows of stones sloping alternately right and left. Their western-end towers contained a priest's room looking onto the nave, and a belfry for the bells.

Look for carvings and symbols of pagan fertility cults. Early priests knew they would have to woo pagans away from their beliefs cautiously. Pope Gregory the Great wrote to a leading missionary in 601:

Destroy the idols; purify the buildings with holy water; set relics there; and let them become temples of the true God. So the people will have no need to change their places of concourse, and where of old they were wont to sacrifice cattle to demons, thither let them continue to resort on the day of the saint to whom the church is dedicated, and slay their beasts no longer as a sacrifice, but for a social meal in honour of Him whom they now worship.

Thus not only did churches get built on pagan sites with their powerful religious links (for example, Rudston church, Yorkshire, stands in a circular churchyard marked by stone monoliths which suggest a pre-Christian religious site), but they also included pagan symbols. Paganism was not left so much as a rival faith but absorbed and conquered by a new one.

In Anglo-Saxon times the new Christian religion was organised on a missionary basis centring on *minsters*. Their success led to the need for a network of private chapels called *oratories* being opened in the surrounding districts. By the end of the eighth century, these private estate chapels were common, but no proper churches were being built because the minsters could not afford

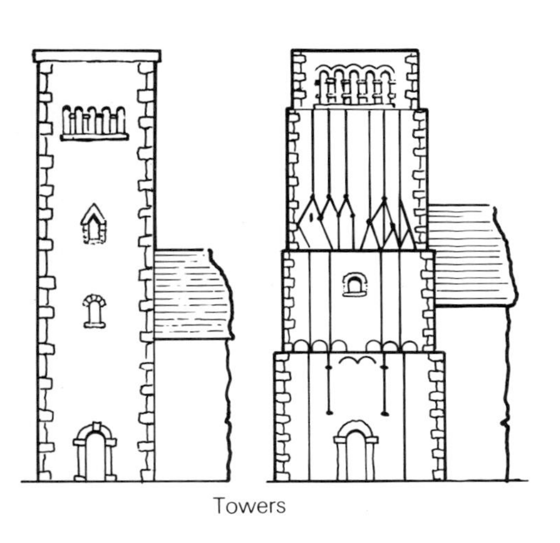

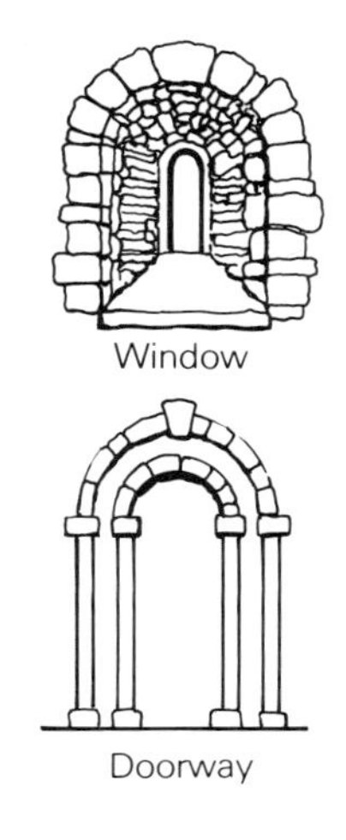

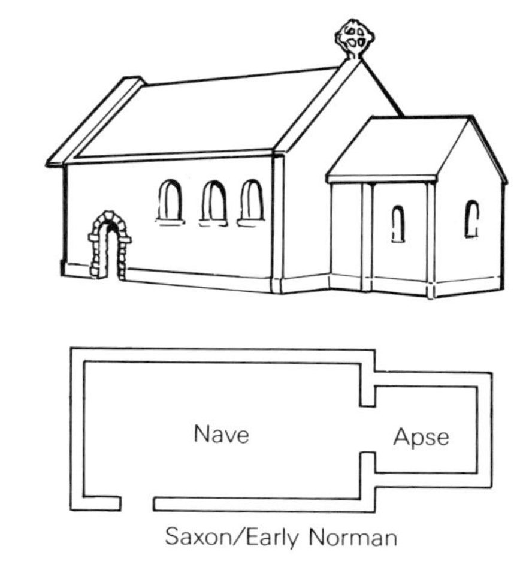

Saxon church architecture

to supply each village with a priest. In the ninth century just when the spread of Christianity meant that more priests were available, Viking raids led to the minsters going bankrupt. This, in turn, resulted in local squires showing off their importance by building *manorial* churches, which served as the first parish churches.

Ownership of the church gave the local squire the right (*advowson*) to appoint its priest and to take a share of the church taxes (*tithes*, see page 25). The manorial church in effect became part of his property. These churches were also unlikely to collapse as the minsters had done because they had the tithes to support them. The collecting of the tithes meant that the boundaries of the collecting area had to be fixed, and thus parish boundaries were laid down.

All these developments are to be found in the way parish churches came to be built, and explains their basic design. See if you can identify the developments. Originally only a small room, which could be called a *chapel*, *chancel*, or *apse*, was needed for the priest to take services, and to this was added a larger room (*nave*) for the local people to be present. This layout was called *cellular linear*. In contrast, the larger minsters were arranged on the *cellular transverse* layout. The additional chapels were for a saint's relics or burial.

NORMAN AND TRANSITIONAL PERIODS, 1066–1200

Their style was called *Romanesque*, as the way the building was laid out reminded people of late-Roman architecture. Look for semicircular arches with *dog-tooth* (zigzag) and other geometrical patterns as they were popular then. Their towers were massive and more squat than Saxon ones as they used to fill the stone walls and pillars with rubble. Their style made the churches look more spacious. The steeply sloping wooden roofs were later replaced by stone ones. These roofs were supported by pillars that were either massive round ones or rectangular ones with slender columns added to them. Which has your church got?

Now look up at the top of the nave. In larger churches a *clerestory* (an extra row of windows above the line of the side aisle roofs) was added above a *triforium* (passage way). Although most of their windows were small, they

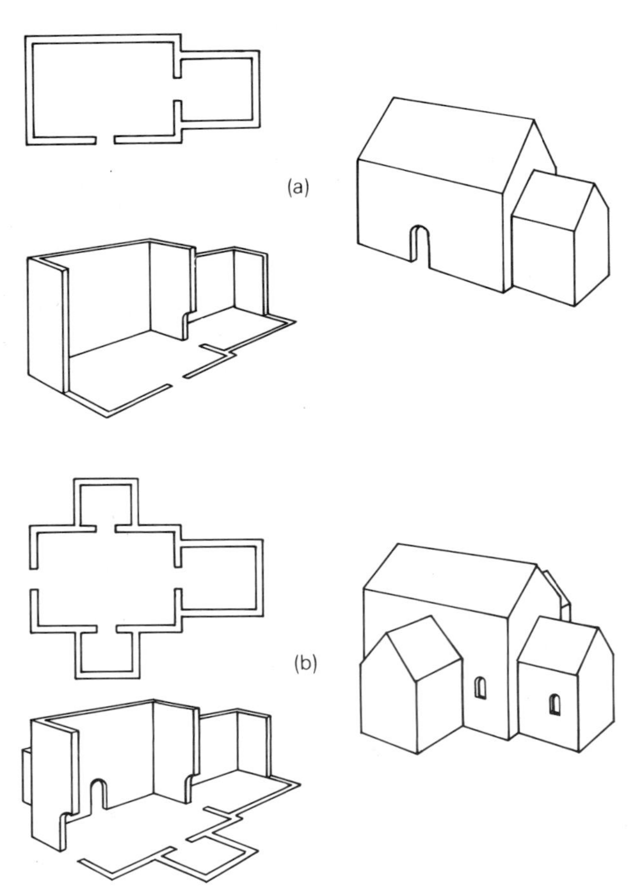

Saxon layouts: (a) cellular linear; (b) cellular transverse

Norman arch at Quenington Church, Gloucestershire, mid-twelfth century.

began to use *mullions* (upright supports dividing a window into two or more sections) so that the windows could be bigger. They also inserted rose windows, so called because they resembled roses.

Buttresses (support walls) were needed to strengthen the heavy stone roofs, even though the thick walls took much of their weight. In the last half of the twelfth century they began to introduce the pointed roof arch, and *rib vaulting*, that is raised arch supports for a roof.

These changes were called *Transitional*, as their style linked the old with the new. For example, Norman mouldings might appear on a pointed chancel arch, or a nave have Norman arches and Early English pillars. So check the arches carefully.

Groined vaulting

Ribbed vaulting

Buttress

Cross-sections of pillars

Window

Doorway

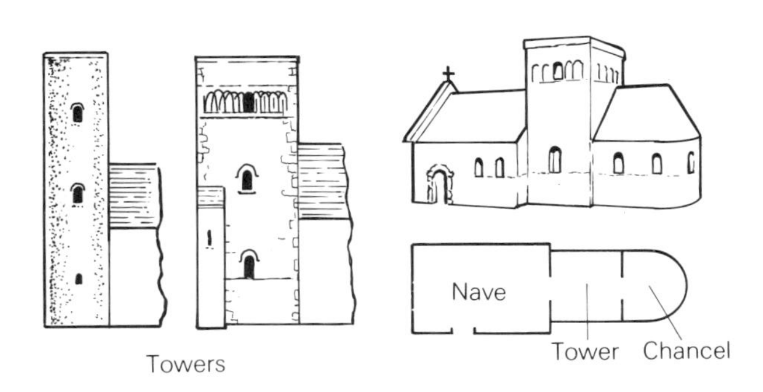

Towers

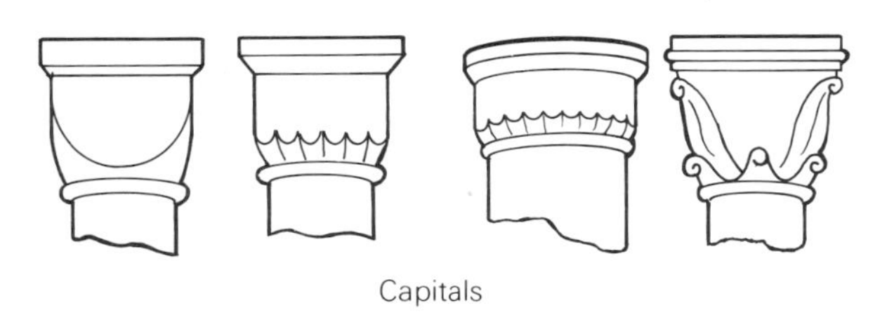

Capitals

Carved mouldings

Norman church architecture

Detail from the Norman font, Southrop, Gloucestershire, showing Virtues triumphing over Vices; here Patience is subduing Wrath. Notice the mirror-writing to emphasise evil.

Gradually the idea caught on that a church ought to be God's (and so the Church's) property, and not that of the local squire. Sometimes local landowners donated the church they had built to a local abbey on condition that the monks said Masses (communion services) for their souls. Then, in the twelfth century, bishops took a closer grip on parish churches, particularly on those not under the control of abbeys. So private ownership of parish churches faded out.

EARLY ENGLISH GOTHIC, 1200–1300

If you want to check for signs that your church was built in this period, look for larger windows and thinner walls, and buttresses strengthened to take the weight of stone roofs. Such churches are lighter inside than earlier ones. Their pointed arches and slender pillars add to this lighter look. Delicate carving came in too. Can you spot any? *Lancet windows* – windows with pointed top – were often arranged in groups of three, especially at the east end of a church to allow more light in.

See if the tower in the church you look at is decorated with pointed arches, or has larger windows than earlier towers. Look carefully to see if you can find a wooden or stone spire, which was usually square; or an octagonal one, with triangles at each corner of the base – they were later designs. Consider why churches had towers at all. There are several possible answers – for bells, treasury stores, and defence purposes, for example.

There were no pulpits in Early English Gothic churches because the sermon was not part of Sunday worship before the mid-fourteenth century. Many clergy were only poorly educated, and so did little more than teach the basic Christian beliefs from the chancel steps.

DECORATED GOTHIC, 1300–50

As its name suggests, you can spot this style in the *tracery* (ornamental stone work) of the windows. Also, look for ornamental carving on the sedilia and piscinas (see pages 28–9), and on tombs (see page 34). Roofs had fine arches and buttresses projected more. Towers became taller and more graceful.

Look for pillars which only curve briefly at the top. Naves and towers were tall, and new churches were more rectangular than before, like spacious halls with large windows. Do you get that impression from your church? Rich wool merchants built what have become known as 'wool' churches with these features. Carvings

Early English church architecture

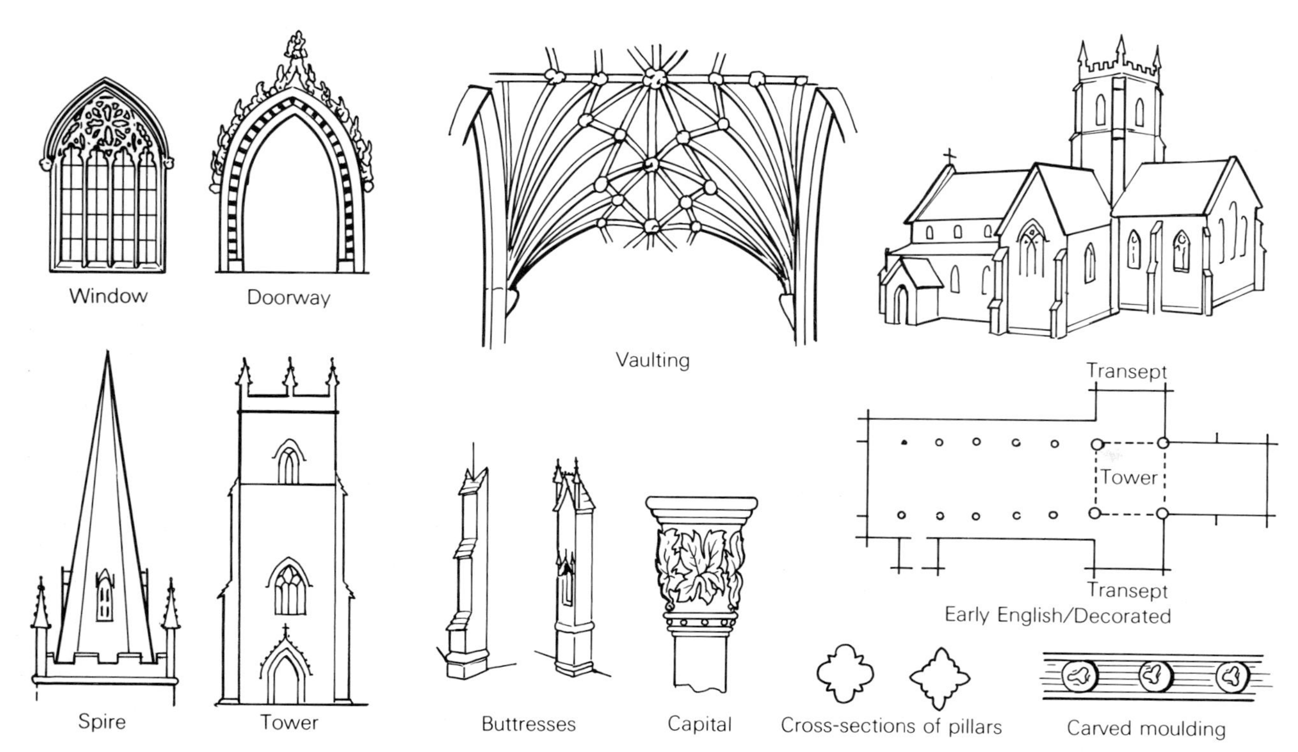

Decorated style of church architecture

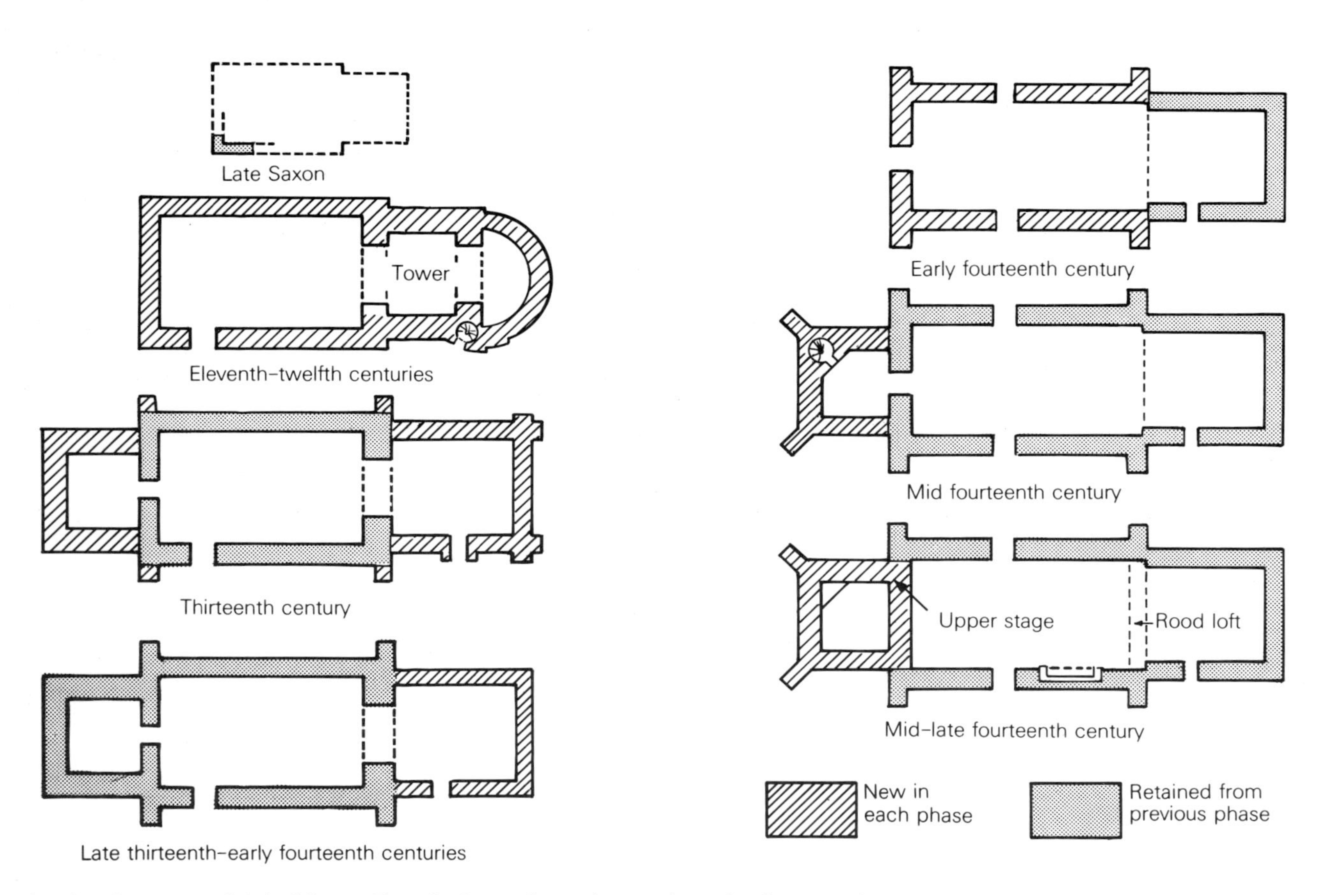

The development of Asheldham Church, Essex, from the tenth to the fourteenth century

of shields, beasts and *gargoyles* (water spouts often in the shape of figures or animals) were everywhere. If your church has some good gargoyles they are worth drawing or photographing. Do the beasts and figures on them have religious meanings?

Fifteenth-century gargoyle from Chedworth Church, Gloucestershire

Count how many small chapels – that is, sections with altars – there are round your church. As the medieval period went on, more clergy became available. In Devon in 1377 there was one priest for every 55 people. Every priest had to say Mass daily, and so numerous side chapels with altars were essential to prevent queuing.

PERPENDICULAR GOTHIC, 1350–1660

During the later part of this period, in the sixteenth century, the *Reformation* occurred, when 'protesting' (Protestant) churches broke away from the Roman Catholic church under its head, the Pope. For years the to-and-fro of Catholic and Protestant kings and queens in England resulted in them giving new orders to their subjects about what to believe and how to worship.

The violence and suddenness of these changes must have shaken people considerably. In 1547 the King ordered churches to 'Take away, utterly extinct, and destroy' shrines, candlesticks and 'all other monuments of feigned miracles, pilgrimages, idolatry and superstition.' The words of the Ten Commandments and the Lord's Prayer were displayed instead, either on large wooden boards or painted straight onto the walls. Wise churchwardens hurriedly sold church plate before it was confiscated. Yatton, Somerset, sold their silver cross and used the money to build a flood barrier in 1549, while St Lawrence's, Reading, paved the streets with the money they made. Stone altars were replaced by wooden communion tables (see page 27) whenever strong-minded Protestants were in power.

Perpendicular church architecture

The closing of the Roman Catholic abbeys meant the loss of income for many parishes and vicars which the abbeys were responsible for. Clergy who held firmly to what they believed was right, had to resign or were sacked. This left those who were willing to chop and change their opinions simply to keep their jobs, whoever was in power. Not surprisingly, church building virtually ceased after the Reformation as gifts dried up.

During the seventeenth century there was the temporary rule of Roundhead *Puritans* – people who believed that worship was best done in a plain building, where nothing would distract one's concentration. The parish register of Keeston, Kent, recorded on 23 April 1643 how 'Our church was defaced, our font thrown down and new forms of prayer appointed.' Pulpits became the focal point of churches when Puritans destroyed many fixtures.

All these changes led to many church fittings being removed, destroyed and replaced over and over again (see Chapter 5). See if you can find evidence of such changes having taken place in the churches you look at. You may spot the outline of some removed fitting on a wall.

Fan vaulting, where the ribs supporting the roof open out in a series of curved fan shapes, was a feature of this period too. *Chantry chapels*, where priests prayed for the donors' souls, were endowed by individuals or craft gilds (see page 26). You could make a special study of such chapels. One gild employed seven priests to pray for its members at St Lawrence's, at Bodmin in Cornwall. It rebuilt the church between 1469 and 1472 by selling the old windows to other churches and running house-to-house collections and fund-raising activities. Towers and spires were also a particular feature of this period. The churchwardens of Totnes visited many church towers before redesigning their own in the 1440s.

Pause a moment with your examination of the building and consider how some of its features were used. *Pew rents* began at this time as a new form of fund raising. Yeovil charged 18d a year for the front pews and 6d or less for those at the back. Men and women sat separately (see pages 30–1). The holy water in fonts was kept locked up in case it was stolen for superstitious practices. Baptism at birth was thought vital in the days before the registration of births. Baptisms were recorded by the priest and very often this was the only way of telling how old a person was, and therefore prove that someone had come of age and could inherit gifts from someone's will.

SEVENTEENTH-CENTURY CLASSICISM

This was the English version of *Baroque* (a very elaborate style popular in Europe then) introduced by Sir Christopher Wren after the Restoration of Charles II to the throne in 1660. This style is easy to spot from the following features: domes above the centre of the churches and galleries running round the edge and rear of the naves, which made town churches look like 'halls'; *Doric, Ionic* and *Corinthian* pillar designs copied from ancient Greece, and *Tuscan* and *Composite* ones from Rome; gilded and painted plaster ceilings; leaves, flowers and fruit carvings on the woodwork.

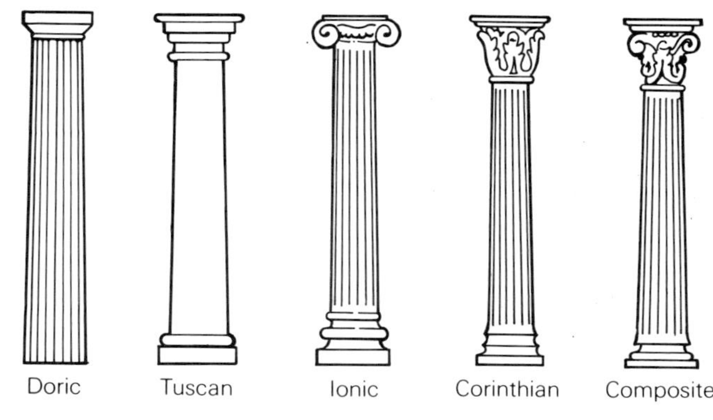

Classical columns

EIGHTEENTH CENTURY

In every town and village people were now faced with choice of going to either a 'church' (Church of England) or a 'chapel' (Nonconformists, e.g. Baptists, Congregationalists, Methodists). Rival buildings and organisations were now permitted, as rulers had given up dictating how people should worship. Competition followed. While rural churches still had congregations reflecting the whole community, town churches tended to attract the better off, leaving chapels to cater for the workers. Often this was because the opening of new chapels only needed magistrates' permission whereas the setting up of a new parish church required a private Act of Parliament as its boundaries would encroach on existing parishes. Thus in the new industrial towns, chapels could spring up easily, while a single parish church had to cope with a huge population.

Competition meant that a good sermon from a prominent pulpit was essential. If your church is oblong, rather than in the shape of a cross, it was because it was designed as a 'preaching box'. Galleries were fitted to pack in large congregations. Three-deck pulpits were introduced (see pages 16 and 28). However, lengthy sermons meant that 'wakers' had to be appointed to prod anyone who fell asleep! If the pulpit is clearly a more important feature than the altar in your church, the building was designed primarily for preaching rather than communion services. Congregational singing gradually came in, with unrobed choirs and orchestras in the gallery. When Frampton-upon-Severn in Gloucestershire established its 'Dads' Army' to face the threat of Napoleon, care was taken to choose instruments which could be used in church or on the parade ground.

Frampton Volunteer Corps' instrument list, 1798

4 Clarinets	2 French Horns
2 Bassoons	1 Base Drum

Look for evidence that churches reflected the class structure of their day. The squire had his pew with sofa, fireplace and sherry during the sermon. Servants would sit in the galleries or at the back. Pew rents became vital with endowments gone. Pews were leased and, as freehold, were bequeathed in wills. This led to many arguments. When St George's, Portland, built in 1766, proved too small in 1917 it was necessary to build a new church (All Saints) as the pew holders would not agree to redesigning the old church.

Churches were the centres for vermin control. These 1751 rates resulted in hundreds being brought to Thorncombe Church, Dorset:

First, to pay for the heads of	*Foxes*	*1s each*
Item	*Martins*	....
....	*Pole Cats*	*4d per head*
....	*Stoats*	*2d* ....
....	*Kites, Hawks*	*4d* ....
....	*Japs, Whoops*	*4d* ....
....	*Crows, Magpies*	*1d* ....
....	*Sparrows*	*2d per dozen*

NINETEENTH CENTURY

In 1818 the Church Building Act's £1 million grant as a 'thanks-offering for Waterloo' resulted in 230 'Waterloo' churches. Built in the new suburbs of big cities, they were in fact the government's 'inner-city plan' to 'civilise' working-class living conditions by putting middle-class Church of England clergy and attractive buildings in their midst. Such buildings had to offer a glimpse of mystery, splendour and hope amidst the grim slums. Most were built in the Gothic style. The government grant meant they had to be built as cheaply as possible, but with plenty of seating space for all the people using them. Augustus Pugin aimed for 'peace and mystery' by the way light shone through the windows. He also filled his churches with decoration. Architect Sir Gilbert Scott built 700 of these churches. Is your church a 'Waterloo' one? If so, look for features which fit these descriptions. In what ways do you think the interior gives an impression of mystery, splendour and hope?

From the beginning of the century to 1850 the population went up from $8\frac{1}{2}$ to 17 million. New industrial towns sprang up, resulting in 3417 new

A Country Church Interior, *painted by J. Wright, 1790. Look for the 1650 'repair' notice, musicians in the gallery, tattered banners, memorial hatchments, and the squire's pew, near the 'three-decker' pulpit with its sounding board*

All Souls, Langham Place, London – a 'Waterloo' church by John Nash

churches being built, and 1007 rebuilt, between 1801 and 1875. The fact that pew holders regarded their pews as their 'property' presented big problems. In Bradford in 1858 of the 1400 seats for a population of 78 000, only 200 were *free*. An influential group called the Ecclesiologists argued that churches must be built in the thirteenth-century Gothic style as that fitted the Prayer Book services, while the sanctuary, chancel and nave symbolised the Trinity (Father, Son, Holy Spirit). Their ideas led to the rebuilding of many churches, often resulting in pulling down eighteenth-century plaster ceilings and scraping off wall plaster which, it was felt, had 'spoilt' earlier work. Pulpits became less important, as the raised-up altar (which now had a cross on it), altar rails and choir stalls focused the service on the chancel. Look for shiny nineteenth-century tiles, generally brown and yellow, red or dark blue, where altars and chancels have been raised up above the nave. High pews were condemned because they meant that you could not see the altar. Can you find evidence of such a layout in your church?

The aim of the *Oxford Tractarian Movement*, and others, was to make religion awe-inspiring again. They pressed for surpliced choirs in choir stalls and an organ, placed near the choir, instead of an orchestra. Check the date when an organ was first installed in your church. Look for fittings by specialist firms such as John Hardman and Co. (stained glass and metalwork), Clayton and Bell (stained glass), and Rattee and Kett of Cambridge (woodwork). Watch out for many-coloured brickwork, granite, marble and Cornish alabaster, tiles, stained glass and gilding, all sure signs of nineteenth-century work. Notice the passionate concern for details, colours, effects. It was in this atmosphere that *Hymns Ancient and Modern* was published, and parish magazines, the Mothers' Unions and the Girls' Friendly Society appeared. The Victorian concern with death led to elaborate funeral services. Is this reflected in the tombstones, monuments and angel figures you can find?

The Poor Law Amendment Act of 1834 and the introduction of local councils reduced the official parish role of caring for most aspects of local life. In 1860 the church courts' control of morals, libel, slander and will disputes also ended.

TWENTIETH CENTURY

Many of the most interesting developments in the twentieth century have taken place since the Second World War. Bombed churches needed rebuilding, some new churches were needed in new towns, while some became redundant as central housing areas were replaced by shops, etc. There is a movement in the Church today called the *Liturgical Movement* which stresses the need to bring God to the people, as opposed to the medieval idea of people reaching out to God. This is achieved by placing the altar in the middle of the church and not at one end.

Such experiments have led to octagonal churches with altars in the middle, and to brilliant patterns of stained glass. The aim is to sweep away the mystery and awesomeness of the last century's churches, so as to get the Christian message across to a new generation through simple, uncluttered interiors in which priest and people are brought close together. However, some

St James the Less, Thorndike Street, London, built in 1858–61. The church was designed by George Street and built with £5000 from two ladies, to inspire local slum dwellers. The chancel was the focal point, as the Tractarian Movement (see page 17) required. Notice the elaborate carvings and decoration. The message behind these designs was that people must 'reach out' to find God

Chancel and south transept of St Augustine's Church at Kilburn, London, 1877. Notice the choir stalls, and the elaborate decoration everywhere

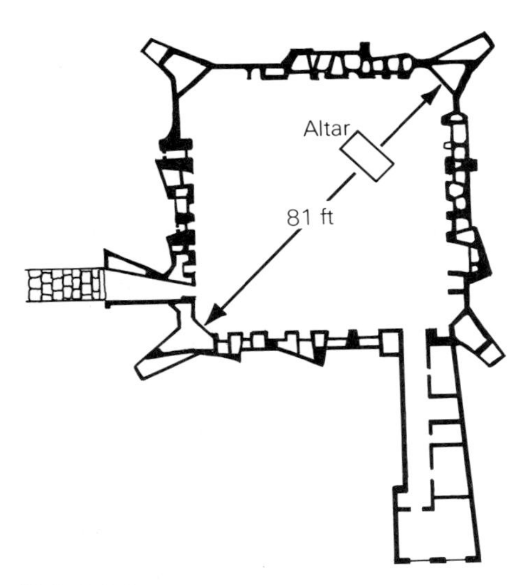

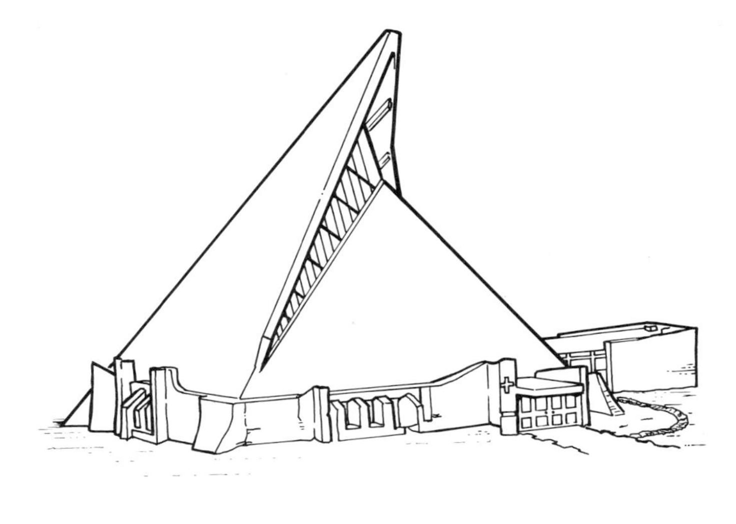

Holy Trinity, Twydall Green, Kent, 1964. The altar forms the central point of this pyramid-style building, and the interior is rough brick, with a cedar shingle roof. The light comes through a large window in the roof

have found these buildings too stark, and lacking in warmth and inspiration, especially when they are situated in the midst of grim tower blocks of flats. How is this starkness achieved by the design and materials used? Which do you think is more attractive in the midst of grim surroundings, a 'nineteenth-century' or 'modern' church? Visit both types if you possibly can and talk to pepole using them.

When you look at some of the new housing estate 'adaptable' churches you will find they have been designed for *everyday* use. Look at this series of plans of a Milton Keynes church for 224 people. It can be used for children's activities, film shows, a boat-building club and senior citizens' meetings. Just as the medieval church coped with all aspects of parish life, so now modern churches are trying to recapture that role.

Another example of a new design is that of Crawley New Town's church, designed by Henry Braddock and D. F. Martin-Smith. In contrast, St Andrew's Church at Sidcup in Kent, which they also designed, was built on two storeys.

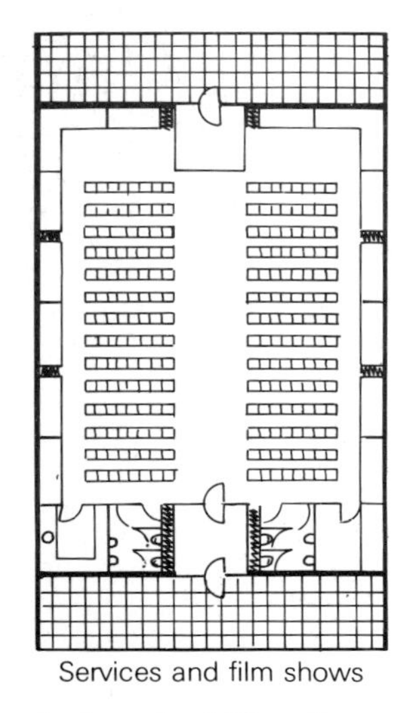

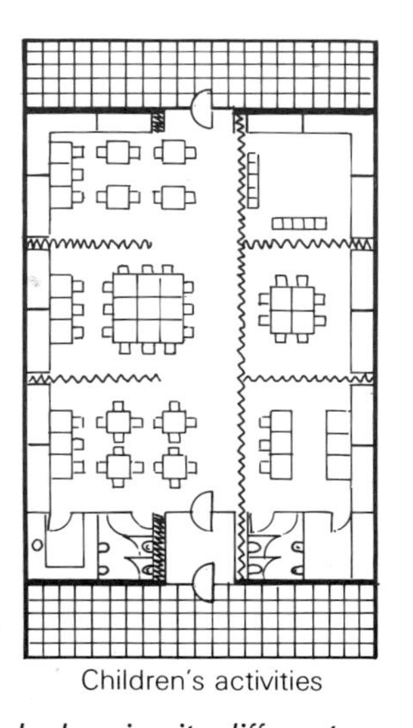

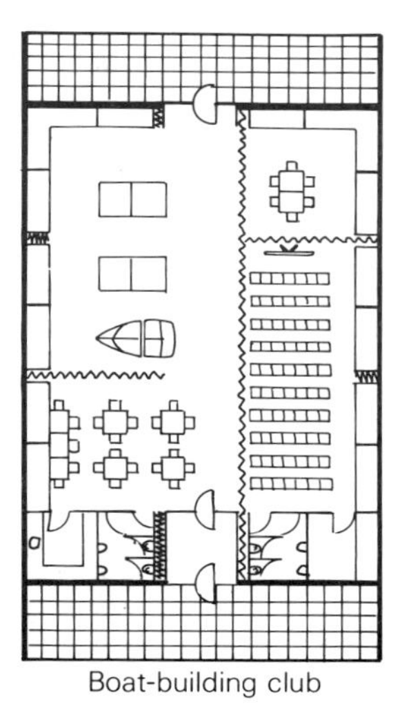

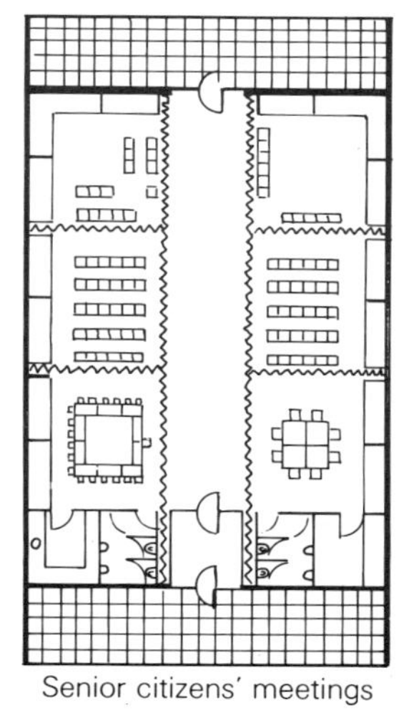

A plan of a Milton Keynes church showing its different uses

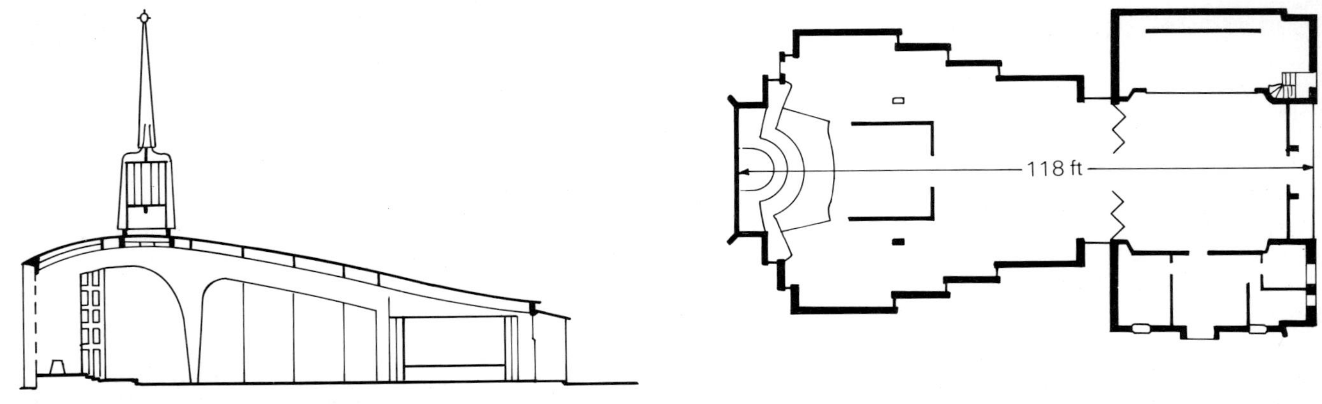

Plan and section of a church and hall at Crawley New Town, 1959

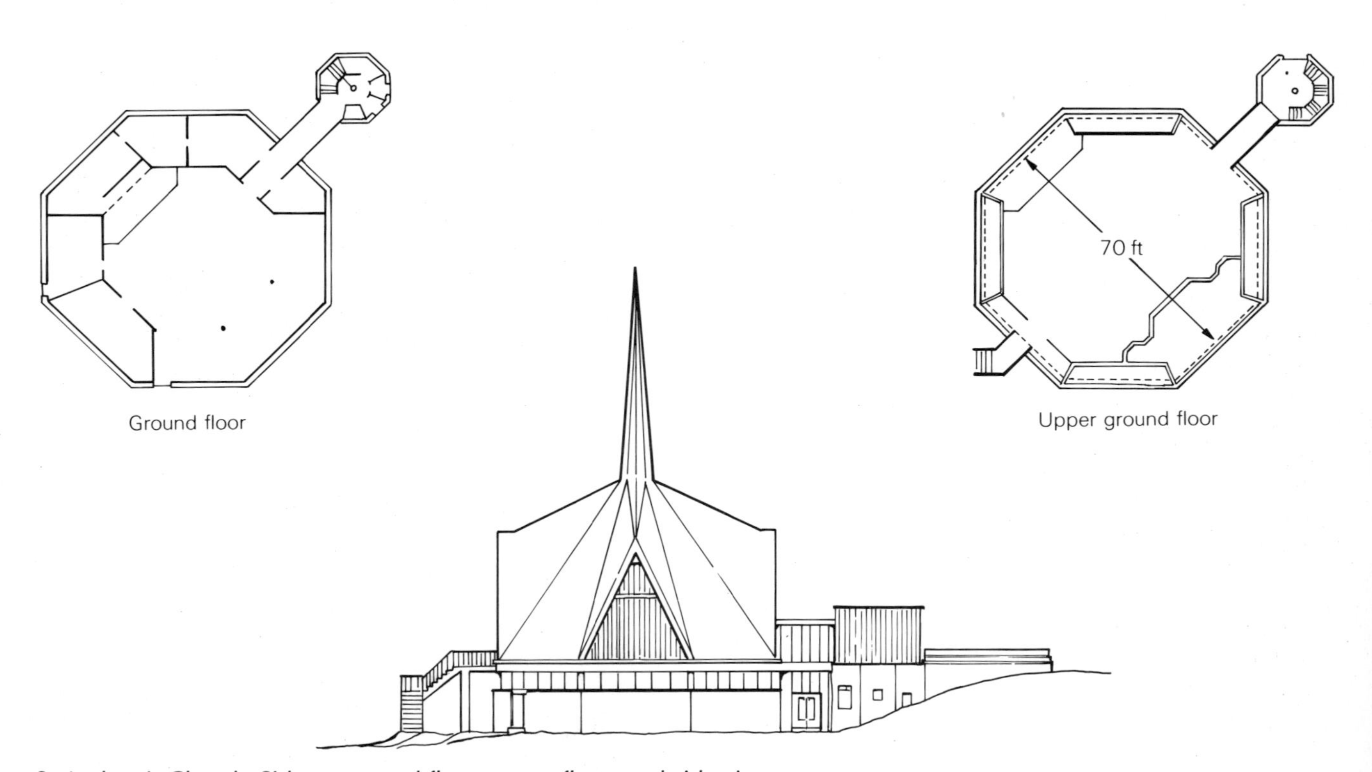

St Andrew's Church, Sidcup: ground floor; upper floor; and side view

See how a chapel can be separated from other parts of the building by such devices as folding soundproof screens. This was done at St Giles', Bullsover Road, Enfield, in 1954. Does the modern church you examine have any means of adapting the building for different purposes?

After examining modern church architecture, design your own church. Start by deciding what you aim to achieve. What is God's relationship to people? How can the two best make contact in services and in private prayer? What opportunities for other church-based functions must you allow for? What administrative offices and toilet facilities are needed? Examine any modern Nonconformist chapels or citadels in your area as they will show how other sects have coped. Can you see from their layouts how their ideas of God's relationship to people may differ from those of the Church of England? So you come back to asking the question 'What is this building for and how is it designed to achieve its aims?' Any examination of a building carried out with this question in mind makes the investigation all the more fascinating.

(b) The Churchyard

THE PURPOSE OF THE CHURCHYARD

Many churchyards cover land once used for pagan ceremonies. This is because early churches were often built inside the protection of prehistoric enclosures. When Pope Gregory I sent St Augustine to convert the Britons in 597, he told him that he should change the pagan temples into churches. This was a clever idea as people would be more likely to accept the new faith if they continued to worship in their usual place. Also, once the site had been dedicated to Christianity, there was no pagan site left for worship. The Normans retained the idea of the rectangular burial ground which the Romans had introduced. Circular churchyards may well pre-date the Romans.

Stone crosses, called *preaching* or *teaching* crosses, marked the first places of Christian worship and it was around these that parish churches grew up. No doubt those who died wanted to be buried near them. In 752 the Pope gave St Cuthbert permission to establish churchyards around churches. This led to the idea of the graveyard. The bishop would consecrate the site and wooden crosses would mark its four corners.

Having a graveyard near the church helped the congregation to think of their souls and the need to pray as they passed the graves. Here, near to God's church, lay the remains of the faithful. Usually graveyards are on the south side of churches to get the benefit of the sun. Evil spirits were thought to lurk on the north side of the church and so strangers, suicides, criminals, and unbaptised babies were buried there.

From the earliest times the church was used as an emergency centre in times of danger. The churchyard was then used for the animals and for storing any possessions brought from homes. As consecrated ground, it had a special kind of security value. In Saxon times, in the absence of a village hall, it was the site for oath-takings and settling disputes. The churchyard cross acted as the focal point for such activities. Table-top tombs were used as market stalls by itinerant salesmen, while players and musicians performed their miracle plays and other entertainments there.

Children played games in the churchyard, like 'fives' where two teams of two used their hands to knock a ball against the buttressed wall of the church. Bellfounders came round and cast the church's bells in the churchyard. People wanting to make agreements of a binding nature felt the churchyard offered a special atmosphere for so doing. Inquests took place there too.

Thus quite apart from funerals, the churchyard was a busy centre of parish activity. Yeovil in Somerset received a regular income from the market stalls which were put up against the churchyard wall each week, and from renting out weights and measures. The annual wake or revel also took place there to raise funds for the church. There was much drinking, eating and dancing. Ashburton parish hired out actors' clothes, devils' heads and wigs, while Croscombe in Somerset benefited from 'Robin Hood money' from Robin Hood plays.

But early churchyards were not enclosed, and animals wandering around were a problem. Parish records recall regular demands that owners control their animals. Fines followed. Later, fences or walls were built. Sometimes the priest made a profit by allowing people to graze their animals within the churchyard, as he held the freehold.

LYCHGATES

Lychgates are the roofed entrance gates to churchyards. *Lich* is Anglo-Saxon for a corpse. The 1549 Prayer Book said that the priest had to meet the deceased at the entrance of the churchyard and begin the burial service there. So the roofed gate provided shelter for the bearers and mourners to await his coming. The parish *bier* (the moveable coffin carrier) would be brought from the church for conveying the body to the graveside. Look for seats along the length of a lychgate for those waiting. The coffin was placed in a three-legged coffin stand or on a wooden or stone rest called a *corpse table* or *coffin stone*. Has your church's lychgate still got a coffin stone? Older lychgates may have religious texts on them, while newer ones may commemorate a local worthy or some event like one of Queen Victoria's jubilees.

Lychgate at Rottingdean, East Sussex

When you enter the churchyard, look round for anything other than tombstones. For example, a nineteenth-century *dry area*, in the form of a ditch, might separate the church from the churchyard. The layers of burials over hundreds of years will have raised the churchyard above the base line of the church's walls so that a ditch would have been the only way to keep the church dry. In a few churchyards you may still find the village stocks or whipping post for public punishments.

Little watchmen's huts may remain from the days when body-snatchers stole bodies to sell for medical research. A stone or iron vault known as a *mort-safe* was a common means of protecting a grave. Sometimes iron cages were put up round graves. Look out for *dole stones* – large slabs near the church porch, where charity bread was given out on the anniversary of the donor's death or some similar occasion.

Punishments beside the church in the Middle Ages

CHURCHYARD CROSSES

Churchyard crosses stood in every churchyard before the Reformation as a sign that the ground was consecrated. Many were destroyed in the seventeenth century by Cromwell's soldiers. Remember that the cross might not be standing in its original position today. It would originally have been midway between the churchyard entrance and the church porch, and feast day processions would have stopped at it in prayer and thanksgiving. In early days the churchyard cross was also the place where public announcements were made. The very earliest crosses mark the site where Christianity was first preached in the village before a church was built. For most of the Middle Ages the cross was the only memorial to virtually all those buried near it, as few could afford tombstones.

Churchyard cross and the Sandys family mausoleum, near the new St. Andrew's Church, Ombersley, Worcestershire. The mausoleum was made out of the chancel of the old church

MEMORIALS

BURIALS

The Anglo-Saxons *sometimes* buried their dead in coffins, but these were not very common until the seventeenth century. Instead, bodies were put in shrouds, tied head and foot, so that a bier was needed to rest them on when carrying them to their graves. The Norman tradition was to start burials on one side of the yard and work across, then to go back to the beginning and work across again. Thus in due course people became buried one on top of another, and so newer graves are nearer the surface. People could not buy plots then, as they can today.

In the twelfth and thirteenth centuries stone coffins were sometimes used. They were sunk almost to ground level, and the slab on top might indicate who was buried there. In the fourteenth century, individual churchyard monuments were less popular. Sometimes bones of previous burials were put in crypts or charnel houses so as to give more room for new burials. By the nineteenth century many churchyards were overcrowded and smelly due to shallow burials, and newly set-up local authorities had to open cemeteries away from the church.

HEADSTONES

Headstones became popular after the Reformation. By the end of the sixteenth century more people could afford to buy plots and set up memorials. Local stone was used, and later slate, artificial stone, polished marble and cast iron. Find out when the earliest monumental masons began work in your town. These were the specialists who replaced local masons. Soft stones were the easiest to carve but have weathered worst. Earlier stones were thick in relation to their height, while later ones were larger and thinner.

Angels were an important feature of seventeenth- and early-eighteenth-century decoration. Originally they were sad, lean figures, but later they became healthy, plump ones who trumpeted victory over death. They offered a smile and tune in the hereafter. When do you find skulls were popular? How does *classical* (that is, Greek or Roman) art affect memorials? Think what different attitudes to death and to life after death are shown on monuments. Look for evidence that the sculptor has had difficulty in getting an inscription to fit neatly into a line or has been careless in the formation of the letters and spaces.

The strong religious feelings of the nineteenth century required everyone to have a separate plot of land and a memorial. But memorials meant that the old system of clearing away previous graves for the sake of new ones could not continue. Victorians wanted their graves to be permanent, and they emphasised this with kerbs, cast-iron rails, etc. Big firms took over from local craftsmen. The wording of inscriptions was considered important. Think why they were chosen when you study them.

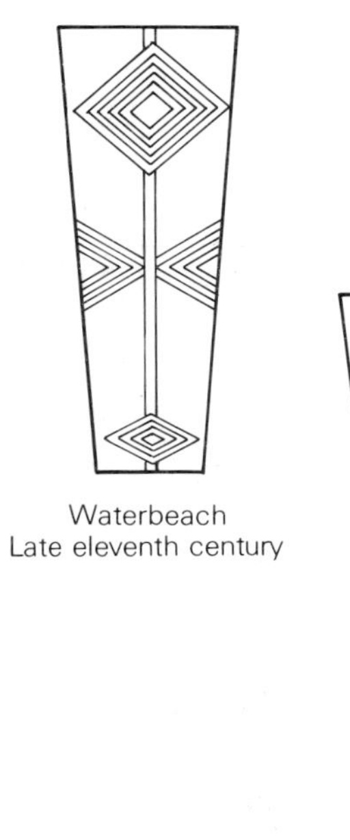

Waterbeach
Late eleventh century

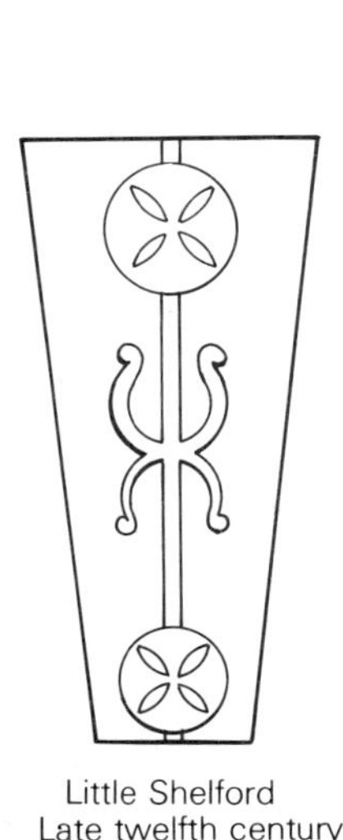

Little Shelford
Late twelfth century

Spaldwick
Mid
thirteenth century

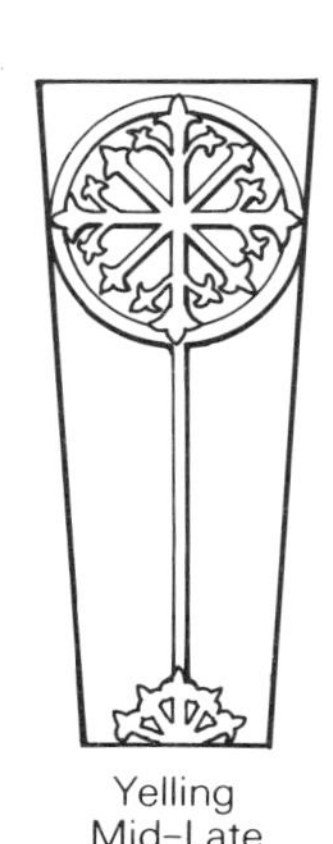

Yelling
Mid–Late
fourteenth century

Yaxley
Mid–Late
fourteenth century

East Anglian grave-slab sculpture from the eleventh to the fourteenth century

GRAVEBOARDS

Graveboards were an alternative to headstones favoured in the south east due to the lack of local freestone. They were long boards supported at the ends by low uprights, and were usually painted white with black lettering. Most have rotted away now. They were easy to move when the grass was cut.

CHEST OR TABLE TOMBS

The idea for these came from altar tombs inside the church, designed to support effigies. They never had effigies on them out of doors. As they were hollow they were liable to collapse due to the effects of soil movement and the weather. The plainer these chest tombs are, the older they tend to be.

BALE TOMBS

Bale tombs are the east Cotswold version of chest tombs. Their name comes from the semi-cylindrical stone which runs the length of the top slab. They probably represented corded bales of cloth when the deceased was connected with the wool trade. Alternatively they could represent a corpse in a woollen shroud.

On page 41 there is advice on how to read difficult tombstone inscriptions and record evidence in a churchyard.

Seventeenth or eighteenth-century bale tombs, Swinbrook, Oxfordshire

(c) Beyond the Churchyard

THE PRIEST'S HOUSE, BARN AND LAND

Look beyond the churchyard for the priest's home (rectory or vicarage) and his tithe barn. He had to live near the church to be available when needed. In 1268 Eynsham Abbey, Oxfordshire, had a vicarage built at its Histon parish in Cambridgeshire consisting of a hall measuring about 8 m by 6 m, with a buttery at one end and a 'competent' chamber (bedroom) with its *garderobe* (toilet) at the other. It had a kitchen, bakehouse and brewhouse too.

Near the parsonage you may find the tithe barn where the priest stored the farm produce which the locals paid to him as the tithe tax. Tithes were divided into 'Great Tithes' (consisting of the main cereal crop and hay) and 'Small Tithes' (minor produce and livestock). A rector was entitled to both, but if the parish was in the hands of an abbey or other owner, a vicar (from the Latin *vicarius*, a 'stand-in') was appointed, and he had only the Small Tithes while the owner took the Great Tithes.

Is there a glebe farm nearby? *Glebe land* meant the priest's farm; priests had to farm just like their congregations. In 1571 the vicar of Langtoft, Yorkshire, was expelled from the church for penning his sheep in the chancel, while on Sunday, 3 April 1670, the Revd Ralph Josselin of Earls Colne, Essex, noted 'Cow calved; administered the sacrament, only 14 present'.

Many old parsonages are nowadays too big for clergy who cannot afford servants. Does your vicar or rector live in a new house, and is the old parsonage divided into flats or sold to someone who can afford to run it today?

The parson collecting his annual tithes. What opinion do you think the artist had of this parson?

The village parish complex at Ashleworth, Gloucestershire. From left to right are the rectory (about 1460), the church (1100–1500) and the tithe barn (about 1500)

CHURCH HOUSES

Church houses were built as meeting places in the late Middle Ages so that non-religious functions did not have to take place in the nave. But in the eighteenth century church houses were allowed to decay, or became inns, poorhouses or schools, and they were replaced by parish halls in the nineteenth and twentieth centuries when a revival in church life occurred. Today, some parishes with small congregations (due to the reduction of housing within their limits and to the decline of churchgoing) have gone back to using the rear of their naves for non-religious purposes. Some have redesigned their naves so that a section can be shut off for that reason.

Some church houses had well-equipped kitchens, as this list of items from the church house at Yatton in 1445 shows:

a kettle	*2 great crocks [pots]*
2 troughs	*9 stands*
4 pans	*barrels*
a bottom for a pan	*21 trendles [plates]*
5 tun vats	*6 table clothes*

GILDS AND SCHOOLS

Gilds were charitable, friendly organisations, often dedicated to a saint, which endowed chantry priests to pray for their members' souls. Bodmin Church had 40 such gilds and Croscombe had Gilds of Young Men, Maidens, Wives, Weavers, Fullers and Archers. In the nineteenth century the equivalent of gilds were the Girls' Friendly Society, the Young Men's Clubs and the Mothers' Union. Gilds endowed schools too.

Referring to South Leverstone, Nottinghamshire, in 1638, an archdeacon noted, 'There is a school kept in the chancel and children whipped there.' Multiplication tables from 1670 are still on the wall of the Lady Chapel of Long Melford Church, Suffolk, while North Cadbury, Somerset, has two alphabets painted on the wall.

Sunday Schools started in the eighteenth century and spread rapidly in the nineteenth century. The figures for Nottingham show how they gave Bible-based primary education for large numbers: in 1802 there were 1860 children in Sunday Schools; in 1834, 7000; and in 1851, 9000 in 38 schools. In 1811 the National Society for the Education of the Poor in the Principles of the Established Church was founded, and soon 40 000 children were being taught in 'National Schools'.

FURTHER READING

Child, M. *Discovering Churchyards* (Shire Publications, 1982)
Child, M. *Discovering Church Architecture: A Glossary of Terms* (Shire Publications, 1984)
Clowney, P. and T. *Exploring Churches* (Shire Publications, 1982)
Harries, J. *Discovering Churches* (Shire Publications, 1984)
Speight, M. *Churchyard Memorials: Their Recognition and Recording* (Bedford Square Press, 1977)
Wright, G. *Discovering Epitaphs* (Shire Publications, 1972)

The church house at Crowcombe in Somerset, 1515, is still in use today

5 Objects from the Past

Parish churches can be so full of artefacts that it is often difficult to know where to begin. Not only are there the obviously Christian items, like the font and pulpit, but there are also the clothes, armour, heraldry, tools, trades and crafts which are displayed on monuments and brasses or in stained-glass windows. Exceptionally there may be an old fire engine, a stocks or ducking stool. Here there is only space to look briefly at such artefacts. You can find out more by looking in some of the books listed at the end of the chapter.

ALTARS

Altars have often been the focal point of the church. Originally they were wooden communion tables which commemorated the Last Supper as a communal meal, but these were sometimes condemned in favour of stone altars, called *mensae* – for instance in 750 and 1076. Stone altars emphasised the sacrifice of Christ for sinners which is symbolically re-enacted whenever the priest consecrates the bread and wine, and brings God and people together in reconciliation. During the Reformation, however, many stone altars were replaced by tables, thus changing the emphasis again. If you check the Prayer Books of Edward VI's and Elizabeth I's reigns you can see how the words of the consecration change too.

Today you may find that a wooden table in the centre of the church is used while a mensa remains at the east end. Altars have five small crosses on top, representing the five wounds inflicted on Christ during the Crucifixion.

A communion table from after the Reformation, Carleton Rode Church, Norfolk

PULPITS

Pulpits were the alternative focal point of the church, reflecting the importance of preaching compared to the communion service. They began to appear in the late Middle Ages when parsons found that they had to compete wth the wandering friars' lively, story-telling sermons, and in 1603 they became compulsory.

Some medieval wooden and stone pulpits still survive. In the church you look at, are there signs of the pulpit having been moved from its original place? If so, is it now in a more or less prominent position? What conclusions can you draw from such a move? One church in Cheltenham has a pulpit which can be moved to a central position on iron rails.

In the late seventeenth and early eighteenth centuries there were three-decker pulpits. The preacher occupied the top, the reader the middle (incorporating the lectern) and the clerk the lowest deck. Testers or sounding boards above the pulpit to amplify the voice, developed during the fifteenth century and were still common 200 years later. In the sixteenth and seventeenth centuries pulpits were fitted with hour-glasses for timing the sermons.

REREDOSES

Reredoses are decorative wall hangings or sculptures at the east end of the church behind the high altar. These show such things as the Passion of Christ, the Lives of the Virgin Mary or the Saints, or the Last Judgement. Many stone reredoses were destroyed during the Reformation, as it was felt that the figures might be seen as idols. In the fourteenth and fifteenth centuries many were made of alabaster or gypsum quarried in Derbyshire. Marble was used in the nineteenth century.

SEDILIA AND PISCINAS

The *sedilia* consists of the three seats by the altar for the priest and his two assistants, the deacon and sub-deacon. Usually they are stone ones set in the wall and date from the twelfth century to the Reformation. Near to them will be a *piscina*, a stone washbasin for use during the Mass. These features were part of the Roman Catholic ceremonial which set the clergy apart from their congregations.

Hogarth's picture of an eighteenth-century church, with three-decker pulpit, organ and box pews. Notice the way tricorn hats were hung up

Early thirteenth-century piscina (left), with dog-tooth arches, and sedilia (right)

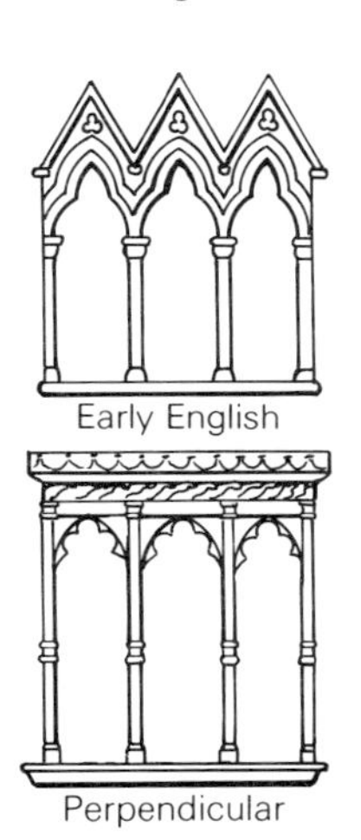

Sedilia

SCREENS

Screens were made of wood, stone or iron, and served a number of purposes. Chancel screens divided the chancel (the responsibility of the priest) from the nave (the responsibility of the people). In Greek Orthodox churches the two sections represent 'heaven', where the priest consecrates the bread and wine, and 'earth', where the people wait to receive communion.

Until the Reformation the *rood screen* was the focal point of the church, with its wooden crucifix (the rood) and attendant figures of the Virgin Mary and St John. Rood lofts were used by musicians and today may have the organ situated on them. Look for signs of a ladder or stone staircase up to the loft.

Piscinas

ALTAR RAILS

When many rood screens were destroyed in the Reformation, altar rails were introduced to protect the altar from dogs or from irreverent people. They are sometimes called 'Laudian' rails, as Archbishop Laud encouraged their erection. The rails can be made of wood, stone or metal.

Rood loft, Horley parish church, Oxfordshire

A medieval wooden lectern, Monksilver parish church, Somerset

LECTERNS

Church reading desks, or *lecterns*, are of two main types, figure (usually eagles) and desk. They are generally made of wood or brass, but occasionally of stone. Brass lecterns were most common in the fifteenth to seventeenth centuries, and had wooden bases to keep the brass from the damp floor. Notice how they are designed to take the weight of large Bibles. Are there any signs that the Bible was chained to the lectern? Desk lecterns often face two ways and sometimes have two levels, one for standing at and the other for kneeling at.

CHOIR STALLS

Choir stalls are a prominent feature of parish churches, and are often interesting for their carvings. Older stalls have *misericords*, which are ledges fitted on the underside of carved hinged seats, for the occupant to lean on while standing for lengthy services. The lay clerks (adult male singers) sat in the back row of the stalls, while the choristers (boys) sat in front. When you look at choir stalls in a church, notice the more elaborate seats for the clergy.

PEWS

Seating in the nave did not exist in the early Middle Ages except for a stone ledge around the side for the elderly or infirm – hence the phrase 'the weakest go to the wall'. Benches developed when pulpit sermons began in the late Middle Ages. It was not until later that benches had backs. Bench-ends were also added later, giving greater strength and providing an opportunity for carvings to be added. Box pews came in after the Reformation and were popular in the Georgian period. They were more comfortable as they stopped the draught to the legs. Sometimes they were locked: Samuel Pepys complained once of having to wait for his pew to be unlocked by the sexton.

Pews could be rented and were often numbered. See if you can find any numbers on the pews in a church you visit. The rents were used to pay for the building of churches erected on new housing estates, for example at Christ Church, Cheltenham, in the early nineteenth century, for retired East India Company employees. Private pews for the wealthy followed the suppression of private chantries by Henry VIII. Usually only the lord of the manor had one, which was known as the 'squire's pew' or the 'family pew'. Sometimes private pews were 'canopied' like four-poster beds, and servants might bring sherry and biscuits in during the sermon.

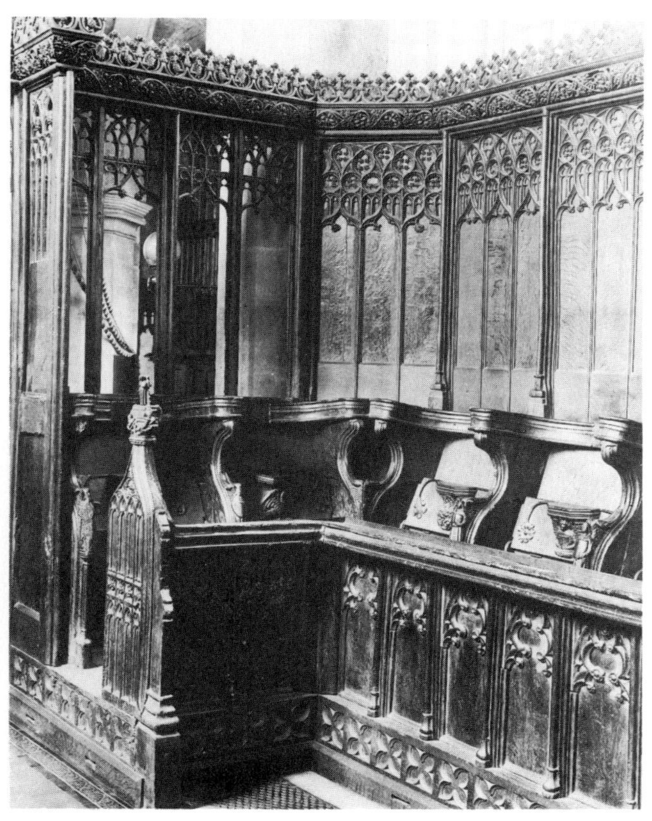

Stalls and misericords, Tong parish church, Shropshire. The seats have been tilted up to show the misericord ledges.

Fourteenth-century misericord, showing a woman sitting by the fire, with a kettle boiling and carcasses hanging

A misericord from Ripple, Gloucestershire, showing a man sowing and a horse pulling a harrow

Box pews, Molland Church, Devon

Carved bench-ends at Colebrooke Chapel, Devon, 1460

The squire's pew, Selworthy parish church, Somerset. It is over the main doorway and is entered from a room above the porch.

Although the occupants could see the preacher, they were often shielded from the gaze of the congregation. The town corporation might also have a special pew – in Dover parish church there is one gallery for the corporation and one for the port officials.

FONTS

Made of lead, stone or marble, fonts are usually situated near the main entrance to symbolise the newly-baptised's reception into the church. They are often difficult to date. In the thirteenth century it was ordered that fonts should have covers which could be locked to prevent the theft of holy water for superstitious purposes. Can you find any sign of a lock-fitting?

CHESTS

In the Middle Ages, when there were no banks, church chests were essential for storing money. For instance, they were used for holding money collected for crusades. When parish registers begin in 1538 chests were needed for them, to say nothing of relics, vestments, documents and chalices. They were usually made of oak by the local carpenter and blacksmith. The earliest chests were *dugouts* or *monoxylons*, that is, ones dug out of tree trunks. Boarded chests came in with the new technique of joinery in the thirteenth century. Later thirteenth-century chests are *stiled*, which means that the corner front and back upright boards are extended to form legs. These keep the chest off the damp floor. Framed and panelled chests developed in the fifteenth century and these were followed by *Jacobean* ones in the seventeenth century.

COLLECTING BOXES

Alms boxes were used for collections in the early Middle Ages before the introduction of wall safes. The boxes were made of oak and strengthened by ironwork. Medieval boxes were basically large logs standing in an upright position. An Elizabethan box, dated 1597, in Bramford Church, Suffolk, is inscribed:

Remember the poor: the Scripture doth record
What to them is given is lent unto the Lord.

Seventeenth-century boxes are often marked with dates and have figures of beggars carved or painted on them. At Tunworth Church in Hampshire, the money is pushed between the lips of carved faces on two sides of the box.

Saxon

Early Norman

Late Norman

Early English

Decorated, with 'ogee' cover

Perpendicular, with pinnacled cover

Classical

Fonts

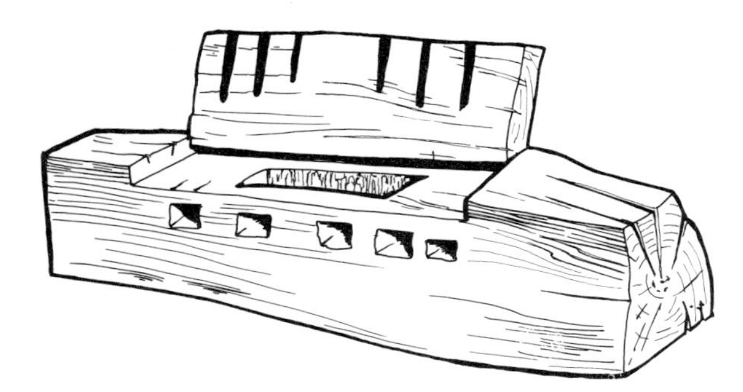

Saxon dugout chest, Wimborne, Dorset

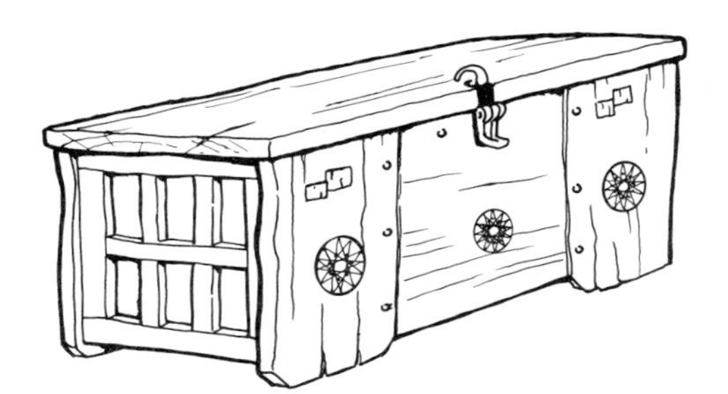

Thirteenth-century chest, Stedham, Sussex

Iron-banded chest, Sleaford, Lincolnshire

WALL PAINTINGS

Wall paintings were a colourful feature of medieval churches. In the days when few could read, they helped people to understand the Bible stories. The wall was covered with plaster and then lime-putty. The paints were made from lime water, skim-milk and some pigments. Unfortunately, few of these paintings survive today.

Fifteenth-century wall painting, Pickering, North Yorkshire

STAINED-GLASS WINDOWS

In early stained-glass windows, the glass was coloured right the way through, but by the fifteenth century it was sometimes merely 'flashed', or given a coating of coloured glass. The glass was drawn upon with a dark paint made with copper or iron oxide. The invention of glass 'enamel' paint in the sixteenth century, and the end of pot-metal supplied from the continent in the seventeenth century, meant that the intricacies of leading and glazing were no longer needed. The nineteenth century saw a revival of the pot-metal method with some success. Today striking new windows have been installed in a few churches.

When you look at a church, watch out for wall paintings and stained-glass windows which stress that judgement and destiny are unavoidable. Think how such visual aids would have affected the illiterate members of the congregation. Why do you think stained-glass windows have remained such a popular feature of churches for so many years?

MEMORIALS

There are often as many memorials inside the parish church as outside. In the Middle Ages important families sometimes had a chantry chapel where priests would say Masses for their souls. Taken in groups, monuments can tell you a lot about the type of congregation the church had. For example, Christ Church, Cheltenham, contains numerous plaques to those who died in the service of the East India Company, many of whom died out in India but whose parents had retired from service there to Cheltenham.

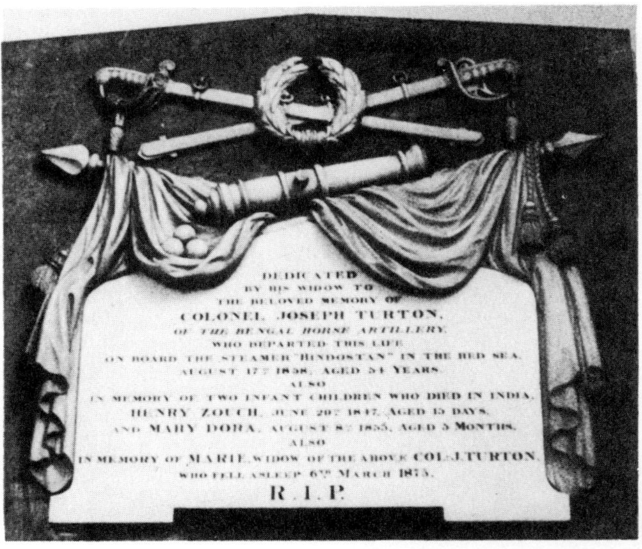

Colonel J. Turton's memorial, Christ Church, Cheltenham, Gloucestershire

TOMBS AND COFFINS

In the twelfth and thirteenth centuries stone coffins were covered by a slab which was often cut with a cross and the symbols of the person's rank or job. Thus a sword and shield marked a knight, while a pair of shears or a fish indicated different kinds of tradesman. These covers were often flush with the floor, with the coffins below ground. At first only clergy were buried in the church but later wealthy people were too. A memorial inside the church might still mean that the body was buried in the churchyard.

By the thirteenth century, effigies were being carved on the covers, and this led to table or altar tombs which were painted and gilded. By the fourteenth century, tombs were sometimes set in recesses in the wall, with canopies over them. The master mason ceased to be the

One of the sixteenth-century Gospel story windows in Fairford Church, Gloucestershire

A widow watching a tombstone being prepared

craftsman involved as those specialising in alabaster carvings took over. Figures became less stiff and different poses came to be used. In the fifteenth and sixteenth centuries 'weepers' were added on the sides, that is small figures of the person's family in mourning. Marble was used from the seventeenth century. Figures like Truth, Victory or Fame, rather than angels, were carved on the tomb to wait upon the deceased. *Hatchments*, showing family coats of arms, were common in the eighteenth century. Watch out for these features when you visit a parish church.

Hatchment of Sir Thomas Samwell (died 1757), Upton, Northamptonshire

The Skinner family, Ledbury, Herefordshire, 1616. Notice the gown worn by this worthy tradesman, the baby between the couple, and their children below

BRASSES

Brasses, dating from the thirteenth to the eighteenth century, were another important form of memorial. They provide valuable evidence about armour and civilian dress. Knights, priests and merchants particularly favoured these memorials. Brass rubbing is an enjoyable hobby today but some churches do not want the originals copied as it may damage them. Reproduction brasses are available in some places for rubbing.

FIREFIGHTING EQUIPMENT

This is still to be found in some churches, such as Puddletown and Bere Regis in Dorset. The church-wardens of Cerne Abbas, Dorset, listed expenditures on their fire engine in 1753:

For oiling the pipe of the Engine	*1s 6d*
For oil and Cleaning of the Engine	*1s 6d*

Brass of Revd William Ermyn (died 1401), Castle Ashby, Northamptonshire. His cope is embroidered with saints

Canvas fire buckets kept by Sun Insurance Co. in Puddleton Church, Dorset

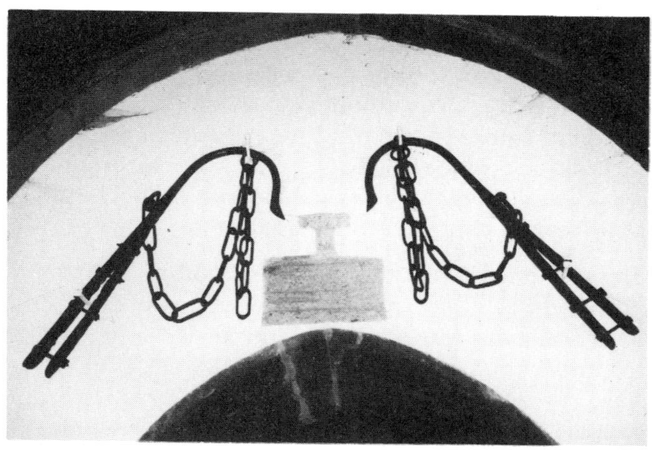

Chains for attaching to poles to pull down burning thatch, c.1600, still in the porch of Bere Regis Church, Dorset

FURTHER READING

Cook, M. *Discovering Brasses and Brass Rubbing* (Shire Publications, 1967)

Delderfield, E. R. *A Guide to Church Furniture* (David & Charles, 1966)

Harries, J. *Discovering Stained Glass* (Shire Publications, 1972)

Howkins, C. *Discovering Church Furniture* (Shire Publications, 1980)

Rouse, E. C. *Discovering Wall Paintings* (Shire Publications, 1971)

6 Talking to People

One of the most rewarding things local historians can do is to interview someone about the subject they are researching into. Just as a detective thinks carefully what questions he wants answered before he sets off, so you will need to draw up a list of questions to put to your 'interviewee'. You will want to put him or her at ease at the start, so think of some good introductory questions. You may spot something on the mantelpiece, or a picture hanging on the wall, which is in some way connected with the subject you are concerned with; and so you may be able to start from there.

Do not forget to ask if he or she has a photograph album or old newspaper cuttings you can look at and discuss. If you are lucky, there may be some interesting old artefacts in the house – perhaps an old parish magazine or photograph of the choir in earlier days, or something else connected with the subject under discussion. Looking together at such things may jog your interviewee's memory. If he or she has obviously got a lot to tell you, do not keep the interview going too long, but ask if you can come back to hear the rest. Old people can get tired, and they might think of something more to tell you by the time you return. (Incidentally, it might be a nice idea to offer to do a bit of gardening or an errand for them, in return for giving you their time. Do not forget to send them a Christmas card later on!)

You will need a portable cassette recorder. A battery-powered one is easier to handle, as you may otherwise find problems in plugging yours in. Do a short test recording to check on echo problems, etc. When you start, say whom you are interviewing and where, and give the date. This will prevent any confusion later on if you record a number of interviews. If possible, try to get the whole recording typed out on paper. Then you can edit it down to a reasonable length and cut out any repetitions. Otherwise, simply write down the most important parts of the tape. (Make sure you do not distort what the interviewees said when you select!)

If you are to get a complete picture of the role of a parish church, you should interview not only the vicar, organist and churchwardens, but also old and young members of the congregation. Find out what changes in worship have taken place, or how the building is convenient or not for modern-day usage. What facilities and services do they expect the church to provide? Did it provide the same facilities in the days that older people can remember? Are the church records kept in the same way as they always used to be? These are just some ideas to begin with when you start your visiting.

St Anne's Church, Catterick

7 Putting the Evidence Together

Now that we have examined different ways of approaching local history, it will be helpful to see how a complete study can be carried out. Here are two such studies.

Case Study 1:

ST ANNE'S CHURCH, CATTERICK

After preliminary class work, Graham Berry divided his students from Richmond School, Yorkshire, into specialist groups and they went to examine a local church. Their basic task was to date the building and its contents. Was it the original church on the site? They were not allowed to look at the church guide book, but had to do the detective work themselves. An 1856 O.S. map drew attention to nearby almshouses, a school and a significant *tumulus* (burial mound). These features were checked on a 1913 O.S. map. The central position of the church and the way the houses curved round the churchyard suggested that the church was there first.

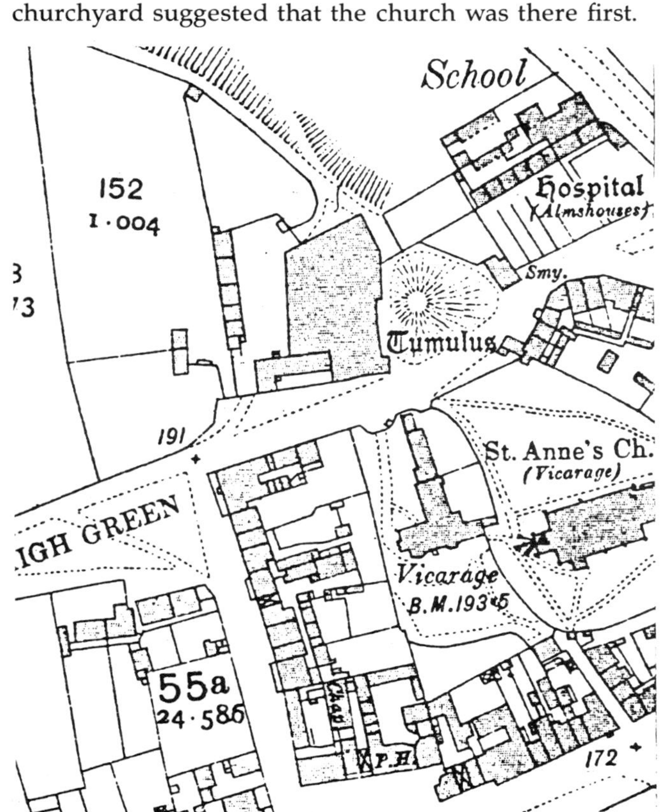

Ordnance survey map of the centre of Catterick, 1913

The earliest documentary evidence was an extract in the *Domesday Book*. Its mention of a church there was backed up for the students by their examination of the effigy of Sir Walter de Urswick, Constable of Richmond Castle in 1371, with its chain mail. They found the type of stone used was not the same as that of the present church. Therefore the monument had originally been in an earlier church. The fact that Sir Walter's legs are now incomplete, and the dog on which they once rested now oddly faces the wall, confirmed this.

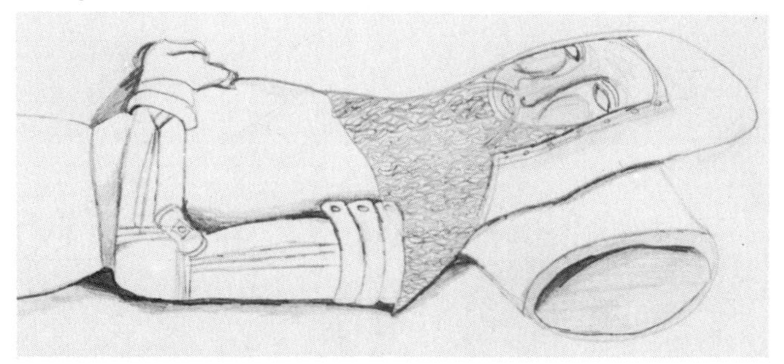

A drawing by a student of part of Sir Walter de Urswick's tomb

The group rubbing the de Burgh brasses went on to find documentary evidence in the county record office of a contract in 1412. In it Lady Catherine de Burgh and her son agreed with Richard of Cracal, the master mason, to rebuild the church for 170 marks (about £115). He was to use, among others, that stone belonging to the burnt-down Saxon church. Richard was given until 1415 to finish the work, unless delayed by war or pestilence. The present church's perpendicular arches and windows confirmed this as the period when the church was built.

On the wall of the chancel, students found a memorial tablet to the Revd Michael Syddall (vicar, 1649–58). Look at his will on page 40. The Michael Syddall School still flourishes in a new building, but council houses have been built on the site of the almshouses. This bequest emphasised the wide role of the church in those days. It turned out that Michael Syddall was a Royalist and grateful for Catterick employing him during the Commonwealth, when Royalists were out of favour.

Reports, drawings, brass rubbings and models were produced to complete the project, which clearly showed the connection between the church and the local community.

Students recording facts from Revd Michael Syddall's memorial. Harvest Festival accounts for the fruit resting on the memorial

Below: The Will of Revd Syddall

Copy of Will of Rev. Michael Syddall

SO FAR AS IT RELATES TO THE ERECTING AND MAINTAINING OF A

—Free School and Hospital and a little Chapel at Catterick.—

In the name of God Amen I Michael Syddall Vicar of Catterick in the County of York, &c., &c. . . . .

PROPERTY of the Trust.
TRUSTEES.
Free School, Hospital, and Chapel to be built.
Master's Salary.
Widows' allowance.
Coats and Gowns for widows.
Qualification of Master.
Scholars' payments.
Prayers to be said twice daily.
Vacancies in Trustees to be filled by Co-optation.

Furthermore my **Will** is that my Executrices before they die deliver or cause to be delivered into the hands of my trusty and good friends Henry Darcy Esqr. Richard Braithwaite Esqr. Wm. Thornton Esqr. & Edward Crofts Esqr. gentlemen all the Deeds Leases and all other writings which concern the above mentioned House Mill Lands and little close together with all the Bonds for the above named Five Hundred Pounds and that the said Hon. Darcy Richard Braithwaite Wm. Thornton and Edward Crofts after the death of both my Executrices do let leases of the said House Mill and Lands and make the best improvement they can of the Five Hundred Pounds and with the increase of the said Five Hundred Pounds and the yearly rents of the House Mill and Lands cause to be built in the town of Catterick one Free School one Hospital and a little Chapel and to pay or cause to be paid yearly out of the said profits twenty pounds to the School Master and three pounds six shillings and eight pence a piece to six poor widows for their yearly maintenance in the said Hospital and in case the aforesaid Rents and increase of Five Hundred Pounds amount to more than Forty pounds my will is that the overplus of the said monies shall be converted to the use of the poor widows only for buying of them coats and gowns. Furthermore my Will is that when the aforesaid Free School Hospital and Chapel are builded upon such a plot of ground as the above named Mr. Hon. Darcy, Mr. Richard Braithwaite, Mr. Wm. Thornton, and Mr. Edward Crofts shall think fit to buy and purchase for that purpose. Then the said four gentlemen do make choice of an able School Master that hath been trained up in the University and is well versed in the Latin and Greek tongues to teach and instruct in the said tongues all the children of the parents inhabiting and dwelling within the Parish of Catterick freely and without taking any wages more than five shillings of every Scholar at his first entrance and likewise to perform the duty of prayer every day morning and evening and cause the widows and scholars to repair duly to the Chapel at the said times when the said religious exercise is to be performed. The widows to be put into the aforesaid Hospital shall be only such as have inhabited and dwelt and do at the time of election inhabit and dwell in the towns of Catterick, Tunstall, West Appleton, Hipswell, Colburn, and the part of Scotton which is in the parish of Catterick. Lastly my will is that when anyone of the four above named gentlemen Mr. Hon. Darcy, Mr. Richard Braithwaite, Mr. Wm. Thornton, and Mr. Edward Crofts shall be taken away by death that then the other three which are living do within the space of ten days or sooner make choice of another gentleman of known integrity to join with them and that upon the same occasion the like be done from time to time. This is my whole and last Will and Testament. In witness, &c.

MICHAEL SYDDALL.

Dated January 3rd, 1658
Witnesses were

FRANCIS BAINBRIDGE
ROBERT KITCHIN
EDWARD CROFTS

This Will was exhibited and proved in Court February 10th, 1658.

Case Study 2:

ORMESBY CHURCHYARD

Under the guidance of Mrs Carole Brown, students from Nunthorpe School, Cleveland, were sent out armed with instructions and a handful of *Grave Memorial Recording Forms*. They had to examine a graveyard and relate it to the community's history, as well as linking it with documentary evidence. Each group examined 6–8 gravestones. They had to map and number the gravestones and fill in a form for each one.

They were told how to read illegible inscriptions:

(a) reflecting the sunlight on to the stone using a mirror
(b) covering the stone with a blanket and using a torch
(c) rubbing wet grass over the stone
(d) pressing tinfoil over the surface and rubbing
(e) taking wax rubbings – using different colours.

On page 42 is the record which Kate Overy made for one stone. Notice that the stone has been photographed and a rubbing of it made.

Back in class, the students checked to see if other stones belonged to the same family and how long the family had been in the parish. Overall checks were made for evidence of immigration, and the average age of death was calculated for different periods. they had to see if there were any seasonal peaks for death as well as anything noticeable about the size of families, infant mortality, age of marriage, epidemics, causes of death and occupations. Parish records, such as the burial records and census returns helped them.

One thing you can do is a check on the change in Christian names used in different periods. In the seventeenth century puritans liked to call their children Charity, Joy, Hope and Love. Here is part of an analysis for Aberford in Yorkshire, showing the most popular names in given periods. How many are Biblical names, and how many are named after members of the royal family?

	1540–52		
	Boys		*Girls*
1st	Thomas	1st =	Alice
2nd	John		Elizabeth
3rd =	William		Anne
	Richard		Margaret
	1594–1601		
	Boys		*Girls*
1st	Thomas	1st	Anne
2nd =	John	2nd	Elizabeth
	William	3rd	Mary
4th	Robert	4th	Alice

Students at work in Ormesby churchyard

Close-up of an Ormesby churchyard gravestone

GRAVE MEMORIAL RECORDING FORM

ST. CUTHEERT'S CHURCH, ORMESBY

DATE: 10th July

GRAVE REFERENCE NUMBER: 1	
MATERIAL USED TO MAKE HEADSTONE: Limestone	
SIZE OF GRAVESTONE: HEIGHT: 170 WIDTH: 80 THICKNESS: 7·6	MEASURE IN CMS.
ORIENTATION OF STONE: (Which way stone faces) East	
FULL INSCRIPTION OF HEADSTONE	DRAWING OF HEADSTONE
IN AFFECTIONATE REMEMBERANCE OF HENRY BRITTAN OF NORTH ORMESBY BORN NOVEMBER 23rd 1828 DIED DECEMBER 3rd 1883 Nevertheless not my will but Thine, be done. Luke xxII c. 42 v.	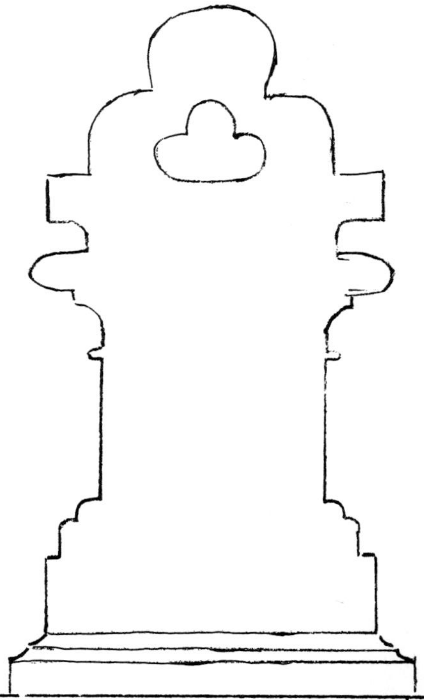
	Tick in Box if Photograph Taken ✓
Name of Mason: J. FIDLER M-BRO	Tick in Box if Rubbing made ✓

Condition of Headstone: Please underline:

Good : Crumbling : Weathered : Leaning
Collapsed : Overgrown

Condition of Inscription: Clear : Clear but Worn : Illegible

Recorder's Name: KATE OVERY.

Grave Memorial Recording Form, St Cuthbert's Church, Ormesby, Cleveland, filled in by Kate Overy

8 Background Reading

In addition to the further reading given at the end of chapters, the following books may provide useful background information:

Beeson, C. F. C. *English Church Clocks* (Phillimore, 1971)

Betjeman, J. *Collins' Guide to English Parish Churches* (Collins, 1968)

Bowen, D. *Looking at Churches* (David & Charles, 1976)

Burgess, F. *English Churchyard Memorials* (Lutterworth Press, 1963)

Camp, J. *Discovering Bells and Bellringing* (Shire Publications, 1977)

Clutton, C. and Niland, A. *The British Organ* (Batsford, 1969)

Dymond, D. *Writing a Church Guide* (Church Information Office, 1977)

Jones, L. E. *The Beauty of English Churches* (Constable, 1978)

Jones, L. E. *What to See in a Country Church* (Phoenix House, 1960)

Lindley, K. *Of Graves and Epitaphs* (Hutchinson, 1965)

Lindley, K. *Graves and Graveyards* (Routledge, 1972)

Page-Phillips, J. *Monumental Brasses* (Allen & Unwin, 1972)

Smith, E. & Cook, C. *British Churches* (Dutton Vista, 1964)

Smith, J. C. D. *A Guide to Church Woodcarvings: Misericords and Benchends* (David & Charles, 1974)

Spiegl, F. *A Small Book of Grave Humour* (Pan, 1971)

Trivick, H. *Picture Book of Brasses in Gilt* (John Baker, 1971)

Index